S0-BOG-376

Editor
Valerie Walkerdine (University of
    Western Sydney)
Email: v.walkerdine@uws.edu.au

Editorial Assistant
Amanda Little
Email: ijcp@uws.edu.au

Book Reviews Editors
Dr Lisa Blackman
Dept of Media and
    Communications,
Goldsmith's College, University of
    London,
London SE14 6NW. UK
Email: coa01lb@gold.ac.uk

Professor Wendy Hollway
Head of Psychology
Faculty of Social Sciences,
The Open University
Milton Keynes
MK7 6AA, UK
Email: w.hollway@open.ac.uk

Associate Editors
Australasia
Ben Bradley (Charles Sturt
    University)
Ann Game (University of New
    South Wales)
Nicola Gavey (University of
    Auckland)
John Kaye (University of Adelaide)
Sue Kippax (University of New
    South Wales)
Isaac Prilleltensky (Victoria
    University)
Jane Ussher (University of
    Western Sydney)

UK
Lisa Blackman (Goldsmiths
    College, University of London)
Stephen Frosh (Birkbeck College,
    University of London)
Wendy Hollway (Open
    University)
Ian Parker (Manchester
    Metropolitan University)
Ann Phoenix (Open University)
Jonathan Potter (Loughborough
    University)
Lynne Segal (Birkbeck College,
    University of London)
Couze Venn (Nottingham Trent
    University)

North America
Tod Sloan (University of Tulsa)
John Broughton (Columbia
    University)
Betty Bayer (Hobart and William
    Smith Colleges)
Kum Kum Bhavnani (University
    of California, Santa Barbara)
Kareen Malone (University of
    West Georgia)
Michelle Fine (The City
    University of New York)

International Editorial Board
Erika Apfelbaum (CNRS, Paris)
Erica Burman (Manchester
    Metropolitan University, UK)
Teresa Cabruja (University of
    Girona, Spain)
Michael Cole (University of
    California, San Diego, USA)
Heidi Figueroa Sarriera
    (University of Puerto Rico)

International Editorial Board (cont)

Angel Gordo-Lopez (University of Madrid, Spain)
David Ingleby (University of Utrecht, Netherlands)
Ingrid Lunt (University of London, UK)
Wolfgang Maiers (Free University of Berlin, Germany)
Amina Mama (University of Cape Town, South Africa)
Janet Sayers (University of Kent, UK)
Corinne Squire (University of East London, UK)

Contents

Book Reviews

Editorial

Valerie Walkerdine

Traditions of critical psychology

This second issue of the journal introduces the incredibly vibrant and diverse field of contemporary critical psychology. The papers and commentaries collected here represent a number of theoretical and political trajectories as they have developed in areas such as Britain, North America, Germany and Australia. It would be ridiculous to suppose that the papers in this issue are representative of all the traditions of work in these countries; but they are of value because the contributors reflect the different places that psychology occupies within radical political projects in specific conjunctures and locations. They show us the diversity of positions that are contained within the umbrella term 'critical psychology'. It is important to recognise and work with these differences, to try to understand where they are coming from, and to be able to debate with different traditions of work in a supportive way. If we do not do that, there is the danger that we will simply have multiplying publications and academic and political forums, each of which reflects only its own part of the theoretical and political tradition at present described as 'critical psychology'.

For example, the work which led to the volume *Changing the Subject*, with which I was associated, came out of a specific set of debates within Britain, both on the left and within feminism. The context was a rejection of English marxism in favour of continental debates and later Eurocommunism, mixed with a feminism which took those debates seriously (usually at that time described 'French feminism'), and a turn to theories of ideology, structuralism, post-structuralism and post-foundational psycho-analysis. Of course this small editorial is not the place to rehearse the particular history of these shifts and allegiances, but I mention them here to illustrate how work takes place within quite specific developments. These ones happened for a relatively small group of people in one place as responses to a particular set of historical and political events. Although similar events left their impact all over the world (the Vietnam War, civil rights, black power, feminism, gay activism, for example), the contexts in which they operated were different. So, for example, Habermas and the Frankfurt School with its 'ideology critique' had a far greater impact in the USA than in Britain; and in Germany the particular experience of living in a divided country with its own forms of left activism produced a very particular form of critical psychology, with important differences from other kinds of work – as well as some similarities.

In order to understand the diversity of work which forms critical psychology now, we need to understand where we have come from and how we have got to where we are; and where other traditions of work place themselves and where they want to go. For this reason this issue of the journal, with its incredibly diverse range of work, presents an important starting point. I want to encourage as many people as possible to write about the traditions of work that they come from, in order to help move forward a mutual understanding, which could take us beyond mutual distrust and suspicion.

In this issue, Wendy Hollway discusses the importance of maternal subjectivity, using debates in both post-structuralism and psychoanalytic theory to move the debate within feminism beyond an impasse in which children's needs have often been understood as antithetical to women's needs. The importance of this work for critical psychology is that – given the development of entirely new family forms and the waning of the norm of a nuclear family with 2.4 children and a non-working mother – it is crucial that accounts are developed which do not place the burden of guilt upon women. Wendy Hollway's paper presents a way of theorising this issue that owes much to the British tradition which I mentioned above. In addition to this however, she turns to both post-Kleinian psychoanalysis and intersubjectivity theory, to develop a position which takes seriously the psychic aspects of social practices.

In some ways the approach adopted in Wendy Hollway's paper is in marked contrast to that of Isaac Prilleltensky and Stephanie Austin. They come out of a North American tradition, which takes Latin American liberation psychology very seriously, with its focus on action and, in particular, on the development of a community psychology which takes as its object the liberation and empowerment of ordinary people. Prilleltensky and Austin set out very clearly how they have taught and researched these issues. Hidden inside the obvious contrast between these two papers are political differences, which come from the emphases in the traditions of work in which their respective authors have engaged. In the particular British tradition that I set out at the beginning of this editorial, there was a strong move away from a notion of liberation. In particular, the notion of an underlying psychological subject to be liberated was criticised, in the context of a critique of theories of ideology which understood the human subject as somehow hidden or occluded by the forces of ideology, and freed by political struggle. This critique owed much to the developments in European social theory to which I have referred, the politics of Eurocommunism and the development of post-structuralism. It should also be seen within a context of many left intellectuals feeling that something had failed after May 1968. This was, and remains, an entirely different context from that of Latin America. Yet each of these positions, just like all of the papers that follow, understands themselves to be doing 'critical psychology'. These different kinds of work, stemming as they do from different traditions, have an important value in allowing us all to see the underlying preconceptions that fuel our own work, and to develop a diversity and plurality within critical psychology.

Within different traditions, because of the different histories and trajectories of work, there are also very different stresses placed on theory and action. How can we do both in a meaningful way? Arnd Hofmeister attempts to bridge this gap with his paper on the critical psychology of learning and teaching. His paper can be understood as an intervention into both the German tradition of critical psychology and the North American dominated field of 'critical pedagogy'. German critical psychology developed in the 1970s with the late Klaus Holzkamp as its figurehead. It is heavily influenced by Marxism, and developed in a way that was quite different from the French-dominated tradition of the particular British trajectory in which I was involved.

Yet, as Hofmeister shows, there are various impasses in the German tradition which can be usefully addressed by making reference to debates with postmodernity. Hofmeister's work both addresses theoretical traditions and is directed to traditions of practice, which it seeks to influence.

The paper by Margaret Vickers and Alex Kouzmin on Employee Assistance Programmes comes at practice from another direction. Their Foucauldian-inspired critique of these programmes demonstrates the place of the psy complex in the formation of the postmodern worker. They analyse practices that seem humanitarian, such as giving employees access to counselling, as regulative devices through which the worker is disciplined. Employee programmes such as they describe are extremely common in Australia and North America, and Vickers and Kouzmin's analysis suggests that, while they appear to be offered by supportive organisations, something else altogether is going on.

Kareen Ror Malone discusses 'acquaintance rape'. She uses a psychoanalytic feminist Lacanian perspective to think about rape prevention practices. In particular, she asks about the production of the desiring subject, in relation to human freedom, identity and the politics of transformation. Critical of the way in which social constructionism has presented this issue as of one of communication or assertiveness, she seeks to locate this debate within a politics that can take desire seriously. This leads her to argue for a possible other practice, one which understands sexuality and desire as centrally implicated in a psyche/body complex existing as an unstable relation. This makes a serious intervention into practices of rape prevention.

Our final paper comes from Ben Bradley, who addresses a very different issue, that of 'synchronicity'. The term is perhaps best known from two trajectories – Jung on the one hand and Saussurian linguistics on the other. Bradley approaches the issue through an engagement with that which has been left out of the scientific project of psychology, that is, the accounting for events which occur synchronously, like the phone ringing when you were about to phone the very person on the end of the line. He argues that psychology's concentration on diachrony has occluded the issue of synchronicity. By moving synchronicity away from the inexplicable, towards its becoming a way of understanding complex links between people, it can be rehabilitated and furthermore can serve an important political function. To understand this phenomenon, Bradley brings together Althusser, Saussure and the physicist David Bohm's notion of a unified field, to begin an attempt to understand collectivity. This work may seem strange to some critical psychologists, but it can be understood as an intervention into the politics of a psychology that might need to broaden its understanding of materiality, and begin to theorise phenomena previously outlawed to the province of the psychical. Bradley does not seek to recuperate them for psychology, but to explore them as important phenomena for a critical psychology.

In addition to the refereed papers, we have three commentaries. The commentaries are short interventions by psychologists and others commenting on topical issues. It is my aim as editor to have a section in which matters of topical importance can be raised and given space. Michelle Fine and her colleagues write a moving commentary on participatory action research with women in prison in the USA. They tell us of the importance of this kind of intervention in a prison population which has increased by over 500 per cent, but they also attest to the huge difficulties involved, difficulties which they approach with great insight and humility. Like Prilleltensky and Austin, they draw on Latin American liberation psychology, and on feminist interventions. It is interesting to compare this to the commentary on 'Mad Pride' by Russell Hall and Sybil Ahmane. Mad pride is a UK-based psychiatric user movement, which draws upon a different theoretical position – the work of Foucault – to argue that the mad want to be recognised as another form of subject, accepted rather than pathologised, in a way which suggests the importance of self-help practices. Finally, Tod Sloan comments on the importance of the study of ideology to psychology. Drawing on the Frankfurt School tradition, Sloan discusses the kind of ideological work that critical psychology could do. I wonder if his intervention might not form a beginning to a discussion on the place of theories of ideology for critical psychology. I say this because the approach adopted by Sloan is quite different from, for example, the tradition of work which uses Althusser and Lacan – such as that of Zizek – and it is also different from Foucault's attempt to move beyond a divide between science and ideology.

In all of these commentaries, as in the papers themselves, a particular set of relations between critical psychologists and Others (prisoners, the mad, consumers) is foregrounded. In Mad Pride, the mad lead the procession, in the prison psychologists co-research with prisoners, and in ideology critique the psychologist accomplishes an uncovering. Understanding and intervening in the very different politics implied in these positions is absolutely essential for critical psychologists. I hope that, like me, readers await a debate with interest, and that there will be a lively exchange of views in forthcoming issues, in the form of both comments and papers.

From motherhood to maternal subjectivity

Wendy Hollway

In moving from concepts of motherhood and mothers to a theorisation of maternal subjectivity that emphasises unconscious intersubjectivity, this paper casts light on the following questions:

- *What is meant by maternal and who qualifies?*
- *Do gender and sex of parents and carers make any systematic difference to an infant, child or adolescent's experience of parenting and their own capacity to care?*
- *If it is agreed that a universal characteristic of the infant-mother relationship is a one-way, non-negotiable dependency, what are the implications for changes in the subjectivity of women who become mothers?*
- *If it is necessary to uncouple the idea of maternal subjectivity from the figure of the mother, how do we understand the continuing relationship between these two?*
- *How does the theorisation of infantile phantasy, and in particular the phantasy of maternal omnipotence, affect how we understand the effectivity of maternal, paternal and other-figure care?*
- *Modifications to a Freudian Oedipal account of the father's role in boys' and girls' separation from the mother are necessitated by the theorisation in this paper. What are the implications for social policy in the context of changing family forms in which many boys and girls grow up without fathers present?*

In the context of changing family forms and reactive claims that 'families need fathers', it is of considerable relevance to inquire seriously into the gendered and moral nature of parenting and its consequences for children's wellbeing using the theoretical perspectives that critical psychology has been involved in developing. This paper is intended to contribute to such knowledge.

I n this paper I try to work out what would be involved – and what would be some of the implications – in moving from the idea of motherhood to maternal subjectivity (which I theorise through the lens of unconscious intersubjectivity). Motherhood connotes a natural state or condition which functions as an empty category into which children's needs can be placed. Critical psychology, at least the post-structuralist variety, has instead seen mothers as objects of government regulation. Feminism has argued for theorising mothers as autonomous subjects with rights. Feminist psychoanalysis has gone further and argued that children need their mothers to be subjects in their own right.

Using feminist and post-structuralist critiques and building upon British and feminist psychoanalysis, I theorise developments in subjectivity and the capacity to care that are made possible by certain characteristics of the relationship with a developing child, characteristics which change over time. More specifically I explore the concepts of maternal ambivalence, containment, recognition and maternal development – all ways of understanding the specific workings and effects of unconscious intersubjective dynamics – in the context of asking how maternal subjectivity is constituted. In this way, the subject of inquiry is shifted from mothers to mothering.

This conceptualisation of maternal subjectivity aims to go beyond subjectivity as subjectification and mothers as the objects of children's needs (or, more recently, rights) and also beyond the idea of mothers as 'autonomous' subjects in their own right (to the extent that the idea of autonomy is one deriving from the rational unitary subject of modernism). Throughout I use the politically relevant theme of who can and should mother to inquire into the boundaries of maternal subjectivity and thus as a lens through which to illuminate the relations among mothering, fathering, parenting, primary caring and caring more broadly. I discuss the effects of these dynamics on adult subjectivities in general.

Women as objects

The lesson drawn from post-structuralism is that we can usefully begin by situating the subject under consideration – mothers in relation to children – in a historical context of power, knowledge and subjectification. Contemporary Western mothering can thus be understood in the light of twentieth-century moves in the governmental regulation of families, in which 'childhood [became] the most intensely governed sector of personal existence'.[1] A whole complex of apparatuses were targeted at the child: child welfare, school, juvenile justice and the education and surveillance of parents. Rose argues that government and regulation were achieved through a strategy of normalisation in which parents (mothers) took on the aspirations, norms and desires which were being articulated, so that 'state' interference was secondary and indirect: 'The strategy of family privacy ... stands ... as a testament to the success of those attempts to construct a family that will take upon itself the responsibility for the duties of socialisation and will have them as its own desires'.[2] This is an example of what Foucault meant by subjectification: a family (in this case) that takes on its own regulation. However, we know from feminist critiques that fathers were not being held responsible for the welfare of their children, either in expert knowledge or in social policy. They were at most secondary while mothers were the main and particular target for the normalisation of children, through the mass media (for example, Winnicott's influential radio broadcasts to mothers), through childcare manuals, through advertising and changing cultural emphases and images.

We also know that in the British post-war period psychology and psychoanalysis have been profoundly influential in this process of 'familialisation',[3] generating many of the experts who produced the knowledge about normal development, normal 'families' and good mothering. Bowlby, whose publications started in the 1940s and spanned forty years, reproduced the idea of the naturalness of the mother-child bond through an authoritative amalgam of scientific discourses. According to Rose, in Winnicott's work, for example, 'the family is simultaneously allotted its responsibilities, assured of its natural capacities and educated in the fact that it needs to be educated by experts in order to have confidence in its own capacities'.[4]

From the 1960s familialisation came under attack from many angles.

In particular, feminist critiques pointed out the way in which mothers were positioned solely as objects of their babies' and families' needs, rather than as people in their own right:

> The claim that mothers had rights and needs of their own provided a standard by which to assess psychological theories of child development. Feminist writers used this standard to highlight the innumerable ways in which psychological theories and models of child development oppressed women, through their failure to consider the other's separate set of needs and interests.[5]

In this perspective, mothers' and children's separateness is taken as a given and to that extent reproduces the premise of unitary (if not also rational) subjects.

Within much of feminism, then, mothers' and children's needs and interests were set up in opposition. It is difficult (at least I find it so) to cast maternal subjectivity in a perspective that does not fall into these still-dominant ways of knowing and does not get carried off in the tide of relativism in relation to what children need from carers in order to grow up moral, creative and productive. Whether a mother has a unique position, whether some elements of her position are universal, and what differences this may make, are unresolved and often avoided questions.

Into this contested domain, I must place my own maternal subjectivity.[6] I have one child – a daughter, now 16 – who until recently lived with me only half the time, the other half of her time being spent with her father (both of us white, Northern English and middle-class). I am positioned in the aforementioned British discourses of mothering, not only as a mother but biographically in my own family of origin: my mother was a post-war, back-to-the-home mother.[7] However, she was plenty more than that description of her economic, cultural and discursive circumstances could predict. My mother did not feel oppressed by her domestic circumstances and neither did she lose sight of her own wishes and desires in the course of bringing up three children. My own combination of career, financial independence and quasi-single mothering is structurally and discursively different from my mother's, but in relational terms – my identifications, investments and mothering practices – we are quite similar. I think this is one of the reasons why I am not convinced by exclusively sociological accounts of mothering, be they structural or discursive.

This does not exempt me from the post-structuralist analysis that I have summarised above: it does, however, raise questions about the subjectivities which provide the material for governmentality and subjectification. Post-structuralist accounts usually sound as if the power is all one-way, as if subjects are malleable material onto which childcare manuals, expert knowledges and government policies can be applied to shape our subjectivity. In my view this is evidently not so: policies, advice and knowledges only effect change in so far as they are pulling in a direction made possible not only by people's circumstances, but by their desires, identities, commitments and anxieties. In my view these require the conceptual tools of psychoanalysis. As Brid Featherstone points out in the introduction to our co-edited book:

> There is a tendency to assume that the structures, institutions and practices of mothering have clear-cut and uniform effects ... What is lost in the process are accounts of maternal subjectivity which can take into account the ways that fantasy, meaning, biography and relational dynamics inform individual women's positions in relation to a variety of discourses concerning motherhood.[8]

These dynamics are forged over a longer period than a single generation. Clinical psychoanalysis provides plenty of evidence for the need to encompass at least three generations in the analysis of maternal subjectivity.[9] On a larger canvas, the inevitable connections between woman and mother are universal and go back beyond history. Contraceptive technology created the first fissure in that connection and now, with technologies like cloning, a more radical break is made possible. That motherhood has histories is incontrovertible and rescues it from biological determinism. It does not, of course, make its significance any less real in terms of the effects that being a mother has on subjectivity.

In re-theorising maternal subjectivity through unconscious intersubjectivity I draw on British psychoanalysis, including theorists who have been criticised for positioning mothers as objects of children's needs: Melanie Klein, Wilfred Bion and, especially, Donald Winnicott. Nonetheless, this psychoanalysis can be read in the light of current feminist and critical developments and, I hope to show, provide the conceptual tools for this endeavour.

Defining mothers and mothering

As I run through in my mind the myriad possible approaches to my topic, I notice that I end up thinking about the welfare of the child; that is, of mothering as the activity that is for someone else (a dependent person). I try to avoid falling into the position that feminists have so vehemently criticised, in which women-as-mothers are understood as objects of their children's needs. I feel as if I should be an example (in my life as well as in what I write) of the claim that 'whereas history has recognised maternal work almost exclusively in terms of its impact on the child, contemporary culture is beginning to articulate the mother as a subject in her own right'.[10]

A further important definitional point is that women who are mothers are not only mothers. Surely this is a crucial distinction. For a few decades after 1945, in Britain as elsewhere in the West, mothering was an entrenched and totalising vision of what women were for. In the communist East, mothers' roles as workers did not diminish their exclusive responsibility for children (as grandmothers as well as mothers). In parts of rural Africa, women share mothering (or the aspects of it that qualify as maternal work and everyday care).[11] All these versions rest on an age-old conflation of womanhood and motherhood (evident in virtually every culture in time and place). Although this conflation has now been unsettled by a whole new visible set of circumstances: contraception, education, employment, lesbian sexuality and women's independent living as a challenge to marriage, we should avoid a juxtaposition of mothers to other women, as if one has to be one or the other. Mothers are not just mothers. Mothers may be employed, engaged in some other productive or creative venture, have relational commitments outside the family. It seems to me that psychoanalysis and psychology, by looking at mothers through the prism of the child's needs, have been compromised by representing women who are mothers as being entirely the objects of their children's developmental needs. This blindness to women's outer and inner lives echoes the narcissistic blindness of a young child to its mother as anything other than an extension of its demands.[12] It suggests a general failing amongst psychologists and psychoanalysts and their audiences to be sensitive to countertransference dynamics in their own emotional relation to the knowledges they were producing.

There remains a question as to how being a mother coexists with these other parts. A post-modern view of multiple fragmented selves would suggest that they simply co-exist – quite possibly in tension. I favour a version of subjectivity that includes the issue of coherence or integration, but does not take this for granted, like modernist versions of the individual. In what ways, if at all, does maternal subjectivity permeate a mother's (and other's) subjectivity more generally and extend beyond the relations of mothers and their children? I will return to these questions at the end.

Despite women being more than mothers, being a mother is defined by a relationship. One is a mother by virtue of having a child. And when those children are of dependent age, mothers are usually primarily responsible for their welfare. The practices through which this is expressed vary and there are exceptions in some cultural arrangements. However, the early relationship between a biological mother and her child has a universal status and the primary characteristic of this is that it is based on a one-way and non-negotiable dependency.

Ruddick argues that certain realities of maternal work (meeting children's demands for preservation, growth and social acceptability) produce universal requirements on mothers.[13] These are not culturally constructed, though others are. Here we are confronted with practical realities that are not compatible with the relativism of most social theories of subjectivity. I want to extend Ruddick's idea of universal maternal work to encompass unconscious emotional work. Within a model of intersubjectivity, this necessitates accepting the powerful effects of children's emotions on maternal subjectivity, what Rosalind Minsky characterises as 'being able to respond creatively to another human being's helplessness'.[14] Who then qualifies? The biological mother? Any woman who stands in for her? The father? Any or every carer of a child? It is important to uncouple the idea of maternal subjectivity from the figure of the mother, but also to look carefully at the relationship between the two.

As Ruddick argued, mothers are not – or at least should not have to be – the sole adults who do maternal work.[15] It would be misleading to imply that psychoanalysis conflates biological mothers and other primary carers, however. Even Bowlby and Winnicott in their understanding of mothering encompassed the primary person who cared for the child consistently and over time. The contemporary debate focuses on fathers in this primary care role. Claims that fathers need to be involved equally in childcare in order to transform the binary gendered identities of children are based on two assumptions.[16] The first is that gender and sex of parents and carers need make no systematic difference to an infant or child or adolescent's experience of parenting. The second is that actual parental care determines the way it is experienced and the effects it has on children. Psychoanalytic theories complicate the relation between a child and maternal or parental care in both these ways.

Having set out a range of preliminary issues which are relevant to a political debate about mothering and the gender of parenting, what are my own positions concerning current critical discourses on mothering? The dismissive claims of some feminist work concerning the relativity of children's needs do not ring true to me. Nor does any too simple claim about a child's or mother's autonomy or connectedness in our emotional bonds. Neither does the position that mothers and fathers are indistinguishable as carers. As for whether mothers' and children's needs are in harmony or necessarily in conflict, neither position is credible in a bald form.

Unconscious intersubjectivity

Melanie Klein worked with a model of love and hate being intrinsic in all object relations (relations to people and things).[17] The earliest experiences of human infants, outside time and language, are split: 'separate worlds of timeless bliss in one ideal universe of experience, and terror and persecution in another alternative universe'.[18] There are no distinctions between self and object, between the emotional experience and the combined external and internal reality that precipitates it. So love and hate are inseparable from good and bad. Good and bad are kept apart (split) to protect the infant from the threat to its psychological survival of the possibility that the good and bad breast/ mother is one and the same. Love and hate are separable – by splitting – but at the cost of compelling acknowledgement of reality. Splitting is the characteristic mode of unconscious intersubjectivity for infants (what Klein called the 'paranoid-schizoid position') and a necessary way of mediating external reality in a dependent state. However, the growing ability to acknowledge, understand and interact with external reality produces a pressure on the infant to acknowledge that good and bad exist in the same object. Klein calls this the 'depressive' position and it is characterised by ambivalence and the increased likelihood of engaging with external reality. Both positions are contingent, unstable and dynamic. They oscillate (and do not therefore resemble 'stages').

These core dynamics in the achievement of relative integration and coherence of self are first of all experienced in relation with the mother. No wonder, then, that the maternal relation is so deeply embedded in everyone's subjectivity in one way or another. This is not the same as saying, however, that other, often subsequent, relationships are not profoundly important.

Maternal ambivalence

At no time in our lives are people beyond the constant, unconscious use of splitting and other intersubjective defences against anxiety. Projection and introjection refer to the unconscious movement of mental objects, ideas or feelings, expelling them in the case of projection and incorporating them in the case of introjection. The purpose is always the same: to protect the self from threats (whether external or internal) and preserve the good where it can aid this protection. Contrary to cultural constructions about maternal love, mothers too are not immune from the splitting of love and hate in their relations with their children.

Rozsika Parker applies the concept of ambivalence to mothers and points out how hard it is for mothers to acknowledge their hate in a culture where the idea of maternal hate is feared, split off and demonised in 'pathological' mothers.[19] This makes it difficult for mothers to access ordinary hate, that is, to acknowledge their less than loving feelings for a child, and therefore to integrate hate, with love, into ambivalence. Parker argues that when hate is incorporated into an ambivalent whole with love, rather than being split off, it helps mothers to think about what their child needs in a realistic way. She takes issue with the way that maternal love has been constructed as the singular emotion that characterises the mother-child relationship. In Western discourse (and arguably beyond) maternal love is usually assumed to be natural and real mothers who do not behave lovingly are consequently regarded as pathological.[20] I see this discursive production of loving mothers as having its roots in a shared defence against the threat (to the child that each of us remains) of maternal hate. This defence against hate reproduces, and is reproduced by, existing language and discourses.[21]

For Winnicott, the infant's earliest relationship (with the mother or other carer) is one of primitive love. By primitive he means that it is prior to any capacity to consider the needs of the other. The infant is solely driven by the need to use the (m)other in the service of its own development. It is 'ruthless', meaning prior to the development of 'routh', in the sense that the infant is not yet capable of feeling concern. This is a universal condition of infancy which, according to Winnicott, is bound to evoke the mother's hatred.[22] Indeed, following from this principle, he lists eighteen good reasons why a mother ordinarily hates her infant.

Not only does he see maternal hate as inevitable (and by this he does not mean inevitably to act it out), but Winnicott argued that 'hating appropriately' is integral to a child's development.[23] As Phillips summarises: 'if [the child] is not hated, if what is unacceptable about him is not acknowledged, then his love and loveableness will not feel fully real to him'.[24] In this way of thinking, hate is necessary for recognition (see next section). Hate (in this example just a realistic acknowledgement of unacceptable aspects of the child) enables both mother and child to acknowledge the imperfect reality of each other and act accordingly. It helps them to separate (without the father's intervention).

If one accepts Winnicott's account, this has implications for understanding the subjectivity of the infant's primary carer. It means that struggling to meet the ruthless demands of an infant (and of course, sometimes failing) is inescapable. If women are to mother, a struggle with these intersubjective conditions – which are bound to be a major assault on anyone's own wishes and desires – come with the job. They position that person – not within a 'discourse' of perfect mothering (though that is likely to intrude), but within a very real set of relations, infused variously by feelings of love, hate, obligation, envy and guilt, among others.

These dynamics modify mothers' subjectivities. It is too soon to insist that the baby modify its demands in the light of the mother's needs and desires. It cannot. This fact is extra-discursive, though how it is lived is not. For example, the concept of maternal ambivalence can help a mother's mixed feelings to be better integrated and aids acknowledgement that babies need imperfection, not perfection, from mothers. In summary, there is a period in children's lives (of variable length depending on historical and cultural factors in the construction of childhood) when their ruthlessly narcissistic demands place terrible strain on mothers, since, in this relationship, they are getting no consideration whatsoever. To bear this is a developmental challenge for anyone.[25]

Winnicott extended this to both parents. He wrote of the child needing to 'test, over and over again their ability to remain good parents in spite of anything he may do to hurt or annoy them. By means of this testing he gradually convinces himself, if the parents do in fact stand the strain'.[26] Winnicott was of the opinion that only the child's real parents were likely to be able to provide and survive this much.[27] Winnicott's insights here were empirically based on his work with English families. Again, it is a matter for empirical observation if similar dynamics exist elsewhere, how they vary and with what effects.

Psychoanalysis, including feminist psychoanalysis, has theorised differences in the way that the 'real' (natural) mother and other primary carers signify for children. Fathers signify differently to mothers because of the infant's initial relation to the mother's body. To this is later added the father's special significance in relation to the mother and her body. The way in which such significations would change if fathers were involved in sole or shared parental care from the start is a challenging question for psychoanalytic theory.[28] The initial dependency on the biological mother's body provokes unconscious fantasies in which the mother is a powerful and dangerous figure.[29] Chasseguet-Smirgel calls this the fantasy of the omnipotent mother.[30] Such phantasies can be experienced in relation to other intimates and carers, through transference and counter-transference dynamics. However, they are at their most powerful in relation to the biological mother. A further effect of the fantasy of an omnipotent mother is the unconscious need to idealise the mother: if she were not ideally good, her power would be too dangerous for the psychologically-vulnerable child to contemplate (and we all remain the children of our mothers). Chodorow and Contratto argue that the fantasy of the perfect mother is evident even in feminist writings which imply that if 'current limitations on mothers were eliminated mothers would know naturally how to be good'.[31] What psychoanalysis adds here, then, is a series of conceptual reasons why, although the idea of maternal work can be extended to apply beyond the mother, the significance for the relationship within which maternal work takes place will be mediated by quite specific unconscious factors to do with dependency and its effects on child-mother gendered power relations. The extensive existence of misogyny suggests that these factors are universal. Maternal work involves more than conscious intentional practices of care. It involves unconscious intersubjective dynamics.

Recognition

In the way that Winnicott's work was taken up, the idea of maternal hate was left aside (for reasons which I have already considered as having to do with the unconscious difficulties of acknowledging anything but mothers' love and the way this has been reproduced in culture). A different theme in Winnicott's work was his claim that if (m)others fail, grossly and consistently, to recognise the gestures of their infant (see below), this will have an enduring effect on its emotional and moral capacities.[32] This claim was criticised because of its implications, which lead to the charge of mother-blaming. There is overwhelming evidence, from developmental psychology, clinical psychotherapy (too numerous to mention), literature and everyday experiences, that this claim is broadly true.[33] For example, the containment provided by institutions, beliefs and cultural practices in pre-modern societies is likely to affect children's vulnerability to not-good-enough mothering. Critical psychology and feminism cannot afford just to blame the mother-blamers: we have to tease out the reality of diverse, complex and variable effectivity of maternal, parental and other care.

According to Winnicott, the development of what he saw as the true self of the baby depended on the lively and authentic response to that baby's gestures. Only in this way can it come to recognise itself as distinct (me from not-me). 'For Winnicott, everything depends on the mother's capacity to relate to her baby intuitively which, for him, means the ability to allow the baby to create reality for itself rather than having it imposed on it'.[34] If a mother repeatedly fails to meet her infant's gestures, this will result, over time, in a false self.[35]

Jessica Benjamin has developed a similar notion to Winnicott's, that of recognition, which she understands as 'to be known as oneself'. She too traces recognition back to the initial mother-baby relationship:

In order to become human beings, we have to receive recognition from the first people who care for us. In our society it is usually the mother who bestows recognition. She responds to our communications, our acts, and our gestures so that we feel they are meaningful. Her recognition makes us feel that vital connection to another being as necessary to human survival as food.[36]

The need for recognition involves a paradox which stems from the omnipotent fantasies of the baby in relation to its mother. The way for the baby to defend against the anxiety of dependency is to control the one on whom it depends. This resembles Winnicott's description of the infant's ruthless use of its mother. But Benjamin moves on to consider a later development where this desire conflicts with a move toward differentiation. If the baby controls her, it cannot experience true recognition from her, because she can only practise recognition from a position of independence. This, for Benjamin, constitutes a 'conflict of differentiation' (one that is re-played in many adult relationships). From this argument, Benjamin develops a position regarding the importance of the mother as subject, rather than object, of the baby's demands.[37] This has been taken up by feminists because it transcends the polarity in arguments about women's or children's needs, as if these were necessarily in conflict.[38]

In Benjamin's argument, it is in the child's interest, as well as the mother's, that the mother is a subject, that is, a person in her own right, differentiated psychologically from the person of her child, capable of recognising the differences between her own wishes and desires and those of her child(ren). Benjamin's explicit stress on recognition, combined with the acknowledgement of conflict in a struggle for control, helps us to make a clear distinction between a mother's capacity to meet her baby's demands and her capacity for recognition of her baby as having different wishes and desires from her own. The emphasis on meeting demands (something I associate more with a 1960s humanistic-permissive discourse) tends toward a model of the mother as object of her child's needs, whereas the latter stresses her as subject, able to meet the child, in its constantly changing manifestations, as nascent subject. Benjamin has now criticised the whole psychoanalytic terminology of subject-object and speaks of subject-subject relations.[39]

Intersubjectivity, separation and differentiation

Thus far I have developed an approach which casts maternal subjectivity in relation to an initially dependent but developing being whose own sense of self is contingent upon the quality of its relationship with a maternal subject in the process of being differentiated. This relationship is constituted primarily through unconscious dynamics which operate between subjects. Stemming from the infant's dependency are fantasies of maternal omnipotence, defences against anxiety, conflicts of control and failures of recognition which, in manageable doses, aid differentiation. Caring for babies in these circumstances means that good enough maternal work involves bearing babies' ruthlessness.

The radical implications of this revision of psychoanalysis can be appreciated if we compare it with Freudian theory about the mother-child relationship.

We have seen how, in the popularisation of psychoanalysis, it tended to follow from positioning mothers as objects of their babies' needs that mothers should respond to everything a baby demanded. However, in this scenario, a mother would psychologically remain an extension of a baby's omnipotent fantasies, not a separate entity. It is for this reason that, for Winnicott, ordinary failure to meet a baby's demands is a necessary part of its forging a differentiated identity: the mother and child can achieve differentiation between them. However, in the kind of Freudian theory that claimed that baby and mother were an inseparable pair, the father was seen as a necessary 'third term' that imposed separation through the trauma of Oedipal conflict. The father may nonetheless stand for difference: 'not the mother/ not me'. His symbolic role is about 'not being the body in which the baby has been carried, suckled and about which the baby fantasises a perpetual, fused future'.[40]

It is well known that this account focussed on the boy-child (whose defences against his forbidden desire for the mother were supposed to endow him with a thoroughly autonomous ego, rather than, as is more likely, a misogyny based on displaced anxiety). Girls' relative failure to separate from the mother resulted, according to Freudian theory, in weaker superegos. In the context of changing family forms in which many boys and girls grow up without fathers present, it is relevant to look closely at the ways that mothers and children have of differentiating without such Oedipal intervention.

I try to maintain a distinction between the terms differentiation and separation. The former refers to the developmental processes that I am trying to theorise that concern maternal-child intersubjectivity. The term separation is used in the context of Oedipal theory, summarised above, and has been criticised for its connotations of defensive individualism and failure to reflect the relational nature of self-development, the account preferred by feminist psychoanalytic theory, particularly for girls.[41]

Containment

Maternal survival is a key notion in Winnicott's accounts of the baby's psychic differentiation from its mother:[42] 'the process by which a subject places an object outside her or his control'[43] and which therefore is the means whereby the other's different identity can be acknowledged. Winnicott, in his idea of the mother's survival, recognised how important it was that she was not damaged by the infant's destructive desires. This relational process is another example of how ordinary maternal failure to meet the child's every demand is necessary for its sense of being separate. A child will experience hate for the mother when she fails to meet its omnipotent and narcissistic demands and wish (in fantasy) to destroy her. By being 'destroyed' (in fantasy) and being unharmed in reality, that is, by surviving, the mother demonstrates that she can safely be 'used' and at the same time that she is not an extension of its unbridled love and hate or phantasies of seduction and destruction.

If we are to understand maternal subjectivity in this light, of the infant's 'use' of the mother (and the changes which occur as the child gets older), this process needs to be theorised in more detail. What happens in the unconscious intersubjective dynamics which means that the mother may survive? What enables her not to retaliate, or precipitates her retaliation? What happens to the baby's negative projections into her? According to Bion, the answer hinges on the mother's capacity for containment (Winnicott often used the term 'holding').

Bion and Winnicott both learned something about infant-mother dynamics through the transference and countertransference in their work as analysts with psychotic and borderline patients. Winnicott claimed that such patients can 'teach the analyst more about early infancy than can be learned from direct observation of infants ... since what happens in the transference is a form of infant-mother relationship'.[44] Bion's concept of containment theorises what he regarded as the most primitive unconscious modes of communication (outside an awareness of time and outside thought) originating in the mother-child relationship. He first described containment through a clinical example:

When the patient strove to rid himself of fears of death which were felt to be too powerful for his personality to contain he split off his fears and put them into me, the idea apparently being that if they were allowed to repose there long enough they would undergo modification by my psyche and could then be safely reintrojected.[45]

Bion contrasts this 'detoxification' with what happens when the other – mother or analyst – fails to contain the subject's fears:

On the occasion I have in mind the patient felt ... that I evacuated them so quickly that the feelings were not modified but had become more painful ... he strove to force them into me with increased desperation and violence. His behaviour, isolated from the context of analysis, might have appeared to be an expression of primary aggression. The more violent his phantasies of projective identification, the more frightened he became of me. There were sessions in which such behaviour expressed unprovoked aggression.[46]

In a characteristic psychoanalytic move, Bion then explores the origins of these powerful fears, which, through the transference, the patient has brought into therapy. These have their origins in the patient's relationship with his mother:

This patient had had to deal with a mother who could not tolerate experiencing such feelings and reacted either by denying them ingress, or alternatively by becoming a prey to the anxiety which resulted from introjection of the baby's bad feelings.[47]

Here Bion is claiming that the failure of this mother to contain the child's hate had negative consequences for his development. This does not address the question of the child's other relationships and whether they might have served this function. Nor does it consider the institutional cultures within which the primary relationship is situated and their capacity for containment. However, it does reflect the probability that this child, like the majority, had to depend primarily on his mother for these capacities. This can change. Bion is demonstrating the biographical, socially-situated workings of intersubjectivity, a biography starting, as it does arguably for all of us, in the early relationship to our mothers. The questions that follow are: to what extent do these dynamics apply beyond infancy and to what extent do, or could, they characterise all relationships?

Bion is claiming that the dynamics of containment are transferred into the adult relationship with the analyst. More generally, psychoanalysis understands such transference dynamics as extending into a wide range of adult relationships (arguably they are a defining characteristic of all relationships). If so, what effects does it have that the earliest version of this unconscious dynamic existed in relation to the mother, with the accompanying fantasies of her omnipotence, the desire to control her but be recognised by her and the tendency to split good and bad when under threat in that relationship? What are the implications for the gender of the transference? Male analysts do work with maternal as well as paternal transferences. However, Chasseguet-Smirgel's analysis suggests that the effects of the fantasy of the omnipotent mother would be visited most powerfully upon the primary maternal figure; if available, the biological mother or one who can represent the mother, in particular, the mother's body. If women are routinely in receipt of such maternal transferences in a way that men are not (paternal transferences are commonly forged out of gender difference from the mother), this will affect their relationships and their subjectivities.

Maternal development

Work on motherhood has been criticised for focusing on the 'initial event' and now I want to consider the effects of children's transformations on maternal subjectivity. In terms of a model like Ruddick's, we could ask, when do the child's needs change or end? At that notional point, presumably mothers would be mothers in name but not in terms of maternal work. Winnicott understands children proceeding from 'absolute dependence, rapidly changing to relative dependence, and always travelling towards, (but never reaching) independence'.[48] The dependence may well reverse at times too. The identificatory connections and thus the unconscious emotional work do not stop at the end of childhood, nor adolescence. I intermittently experience vestiges of my own childlike demands on my mother – who is nearly eighty – which are produced in the dynamic between us. Nonetheless, self or moral development can be seen as the capacity to feel what Winnicott called 'routh' (concern). In Klein's terms, it involves integrating love and hate into ambivalence, facing reality, where good and bad can be acknowledged in the same object. This is an ongoing struggle.[49] As and when a child is capable of relating to their mother in this way, it will change the nature of the maternal subjectivity which is constituted in response. The care involved will hopefully become reciprocal.

Rozsika Parker introduced the idea of maternal development to challenge the exclusive emphasis on child development and as part of her aim to theorise mothers rather than continue in the tradition of casting them as static and empty theoretical categories to be filled by their children's needs.[50] I want to take up the idea of maternal development in order to go beyond the notion of mother as subject in her own right, to situate it in unconscious intersubjectivity.

The inevitability of the child's development is mirrored in maternal development.[51] This is not just an effect of positioning the mother as an unmediated respondent to the changing needs of the child, but can be understood through the frame of unconscious intersubjective dynamics. The child's ruthless demands place great strain on mothers to develop out of their own childlike narcissism. Being used as an extension of a controlling and narcissistic infant's demands usually gives way gradually to a relationship with someone who – most of the time – can imagine themselves in your position and recognise the differences between you in so doing.[52] These developments are neither inevitable nor entirely stable when they are achieved. However, the maternal figure is not simply on the receiving end of these. She changes. Every developmental move (regress as well as progress) is inevitably and interminably produced and reproduced (and changed) intersubjectively.

In this case, it has implications for other relationships and other subjectivities. The capacities which have been constituted in the (good enough) maternal relation are not stranded there. Maternal development is subjective development: containment and recognition, integration into ambivalence. These capacities, to the extent that they are developed, will be used in relation to others. They can enhance our capacities as friends, lovers, team-members, managers and neighbours. As they do so, they help to constitute the subjectivities of those others: recognition helps the development of the other's integration and differentiation; containment helps them face formerly unbearable ideas and helps toward integration of love and hate into ambivalence. Survival (in Winnicott's sense) demonstrates to the other the boundary between their destructive fantasy and reality. These capacities are mutually constituting. Arguably, this is a model for all adult development.[53] Where adult relationships are concerned, it is important that the relationship is characterised by reciprocity in these qualities. The numerous examples where women remain in a maternal position with adult men (notably their partners) demonstrate both the possibility of not becoming 'adult' in this way and its importance for gender equality.

Maternal subjectivity

From the perspective of unconscious intersubjectivity, we could identify the defining feature of the specifically maternal as the dynamic which is constituted in relation to ruthless infantile needs and the consequent capacities of ambivalence (integration of love and hate), recognition and containment which may be developed as a result. These are capacities which depend on a robust sense of one's own differentiated subjectivity. Not all mothers will manage this.[54] If it is a capacity which women can develop (or fail to develop) as part of the challenge of being mothers, then others in equivalent positions can develop (or fail to develop) this aspect of 'maternal' subjectivity too. Any adult can potentially put themselves in this relation to a dependent infant. Preserving a distinction between the term maternal, and 'mother' makes it possible to conceptualise capacities like containment as available, in theory if not always in practice, to us all: women and men, psychoanalysts and patients, adults and (over time) children.

On the other hand, there are specific conditions, biological and historical, structural and psychological, that render actual mothers the most susceptible to the intersubjective dynamics within which maternal subjectivity is constituted. Psychologically, it seems likely that there is a systematic difference in the extent of ruthlessness to which young children subject their real mothers, other women and fathers as primary carers. This will also depend on the age of the child. This does not mean that only mothers will develop maternal subjectivity. Empirical research has reported such characteristics (albeit not theorised in this manner) in men who mother.[55] Such differences can be explained, according to psychoanalysis, because the same actual care (integration of love and hate, recognition, containment) does not mean the same thing to the other (in this case the child), for whom it is mediated by gendered and generational fantasies about that other. It may be that biological mothers, or women, will occupy a unique place in a baby's imagination because of its relation to the female body, starting before birth. If so, this will unconsciously affect their relation to the sexed differences of all bodies/others. Nonetheless it may be that diminishing polarisation in the gender of parenting and caring would eventually affect unconscious fantasies about the omnipotent mother. To address that question more work needs to be done in theorising the maternal body within the framework of unconscious intersubjectivity and in family conditions which challenge the gendered division of maternal unconscious emotional work.

The intersubjective capacities that enable a person to bear the demands of others in the service of their moral development should not be belittled, as part of the critique of a gendered division of emotional labour which discriminates against women – although in some respects it has done. Rather we can look at this maternal capacity – or rather the struggle to develop this capacity in relation to children – as something inherent in everyone, which can enhance all relationships. In contrast to either masochism or narcissism, Kristeva described this process as 'the slow, difficult and delightful apprenticeship in attentiveness, gentleness, forgetting oneself'.[56] If 'forgetting oneself' has unfortunate connotations of abnegation, I offer an interpretation which is more like Bion's idea of reverie: a temporary suspension of memory and desire which draws on subjective resources far removed from the phalllogocentric subject. This is where another kind of communication resides, one rooted in empathic identification with the other from a foundation in a differentiated and integrated subjectivity.

The development of the capacities that I am collecting together under the term maternal subjectivity is not guaranteed by becoming a mother, but the infant does demand them and good enough conditions (external and internal) make their development likely. I have argued that while the demands are likely to be most powerfully experienced by a natural mother (who, after all, has grown that life as part of her own body), an equivalent position is likely to elicit these resources in others as well. While some men find it more difficult to find a creative identification with a helpless, dependent and ruthless infant, because of the history and biography of masculinities as other than the maternal, some men can and do. By focussing on intersubjective dynamics such as these, I have been able to extend the idea of maternal subjectivity beyond natural mothers and beyond women. These dynamics extend beyond women and children also in the way that the effects of ambivalence, containment and recognition carry into any relationship. We are all better off in relationships characterised by these reciprocal capacities.

I have found myself moving beyond the idea of a mother as autonomous subject in her own right, reinstating it with an intersubjective set of concepts in which a differentiated and integrated maternal subject is nonetheless central. Throughout, the child is in the picture in a way that might alarm some feminist sensibilities (including my own). This not only corresponds to my own experience of mothering, but theoretically with the idea of the intersubjectivity of the mother-child relationship. While a mother, in her other relationships and activities, may be temporarily free from these dynamics, to understand what is going on in the ongoing relationship between mother and child requires a challenge to this rather Enlightenment idea of a bounded autonomous subject.

I know that in traditional psychoanalytic thinking, a focus on the interpenetration of maternal and child subjectivities was seen as a problem for the child and a deficit in the mother. Yet at the same time British clinical psychoanalysts were theorising the most basic aspects of understanding another person in terms of the mother-infant relationship. Winnicott's and Bion's own capacity for containment, ambivalence and recognition were not achieved at the expense of their differentiated and integrated subjectivities but rather because of them.

The theorisation of subjectivity is made difficult in the context of current binaries: separation or connection, autonomy or relation, integration or fragmentation, unity or multiplicity, and my understanding of maternal subjectivity in terms of unconscious intersubjectivity requires more development of these issues than this paper can provide. My position, following the Kleinian principles outlined at the beginning of this paper, has been that differentiation and integration go together, as desirable but difficult achievements, and that, in this specific sense, what is good for a mother, or any adult carer, is good for the developing child. My uses of the terms mother and maternal have been impossible to fix, since I have tried to hold on to the paradox of both broadening their applicability as I proceeded and keeping in view the particular psychological significance of the natural mother. Usually mother signifies, as in psychoanalytic usage, that primary carer who is still most likely to be a child's natural mother

This close look into the function of maternal subjectivity demands a parallel look at paternal subjectivity. The British psychoanalytic tradition has rightly been criticised for emphasising the mother-child dyad at the expense of the triangular relationship which traditionally consisted of mother, father and child. Ron Britton has been exemplary in developing Kleinian thought to take account of the importance of the triangle in the child's developing subjectivity.[57] Just as I have included a consideration of men and fathers in the maternal, such an exploration would extend to how women and mothers participate in paternal functions.

Notes

1. N. Rose, *Governing the Soul*, Routledge, London 1990, p121.
2. *Ibid*, p208.
3. *Ibid*.
4. *Ibid*, p203. See D. W. Winnicott, *Collected Papers. Through Paediatrics to Psychoanalysis*, Tavistock, London 1958.
5. C. Everingham, *Motherhood and Maternity*, Open University Press, Milton Keynes 1994, p3.
6. I do not believe that the requirements of reflexivity in social science writing are adequately met in the rather sociological convention of describing one's own identity along the key dimensions of social difference, although that is informative. Elsewhere, I have argued for the use of the psychoanalytic concepts of transference and counter-transference as a complementary approach to tracing the effects of one's own subjectivity in knowledge production: W. Hollway, 'Reflexivity, Unconscious Intersubjectivity and the Co-Production of Data', unpublished.
7. Correlatively, my father was out of the house, at work, five days a week, ten

hours a day, forty-nine weeks of the year, working in a medium-sized family business not unlike that of my mother's father and his brothers.

8. B. Featherstone, 'Introduction. Crisis in the Western family', in W. Hollway and B. Featherstone (eds), *Mothering and Ambivalence*, Routledge, London 1997, p7.

9. For example, M. Mills, 'The Waters Under the Earth: Understanding Maternal Depression', in J. Raphael-Leff and R. Perelberg (eds), *Female Experience*, Routledge, London 1997.

10. D. Bassin, M. Honey & M. M. Kaplan (eds), *Representations of Motherhood*, Yale University Press, New Haven 1994, p9.

11. And in Freud's own family, according to Anna Freud's biographer, E. Young-Bruehl, *Subject to Biography*, Harvard University Press, Cambridge, Massachusetts 1998.

12. It also goes hand-in-glove with traditional images of women's lacks, especially the lack of an active, desirous and sexual subjectivity.

13. S. Ruddick, 'Maternal Thinking', *Feminist Studies*, 6 (2), 1980, pp342-67; S. Ruddick, *Maternal Thinking: Towards a Politics of Peace*, Beacon Press, Boston, Massachusetts 1989.

14. R. Minsky, *Psychoanalysis and Culture: Contemporary States of Mind*, Polity, Cambridge 1998, p119.

15. That mothers often feel primary and may want to feel that way is an aspect of maternal subjectivity that deserves more attention.

16. For example, N. Chodorow, *The Reproduction of Mothering*, University of California Press, London 1978.

17. M. Klein, *Love, Guilt and Reparation and other works 1921-1945*, Virago, London 1988a; M. Klein, *Envy and Gratitude and other works 1946-1963*, Virago, London 1988b.

18. R. Britton, 'The Missing Link: Parental Sexuality in the Oedipus Complex', in D. Breen (ed), *The Gender Conundrum*, Routledge, London 1993, p38.

19. R. Parker, *Torn in Two: The Experience of Maternal Ambivalence*, Virago, London 1995; R. Parker, 'The Production and Purposes of Maternal Ambivalence', in W. Hollway and B. Featherstone (eds), *Mothering and Ambivalence*, Routledge, London 1997, pp17-36.

20. For example, Deigh, a philosopher who is trying to understand moral agency in a more relational way than is traditional, sets up a category, applied to mothers, of 'natural feelings and attitudes' (affection, love, dependency, feelings of protectiveness) based on the model of 'an infant's trust in its mother, in which it recognises mother's goodwill', J. Deigh, *The Sources of Moral Agency*, Cambridge Univ. Press, Cambridge 1996, pp 4-5. Influential feminisms have reproduced this assumption, notably the self-in-relation theorists of the Stone School: J. Jordan A. Kaplan, J. Miller, I. Stiver & J. Surrey (eds), *Women's Growth in Connection*, Guilford Press, New York 1991. Their theory of women's subjectivity is not only based on the idea of connection or relation (rather than autonomy and separateness),

but these relations are understood as basically good, based in empathy. See also R. Coward, 'The Heaven and the Hell of Mothering', in W. Hollway and B. Featherstone (eds), *Mothering and Ambivalence*, Routledge, London 1997, pp111-18.

21. If you have already reacted with irritation or dislike against the use of this word hate, think again. It is only the opposite of love and should be able to encompass ordinary emotions like dislike, irritation, anger, rejection. Yet in our culture it is regarded as too strong: a defence against anxiety operating at a discursive level and reproduced through unconscious dynamics. Kleinian psychoanalysis, in insisting on the co-existence of love and hate, was making a point about the primitive character of emotions in unconscious life, emotions which we are likely to defend against.

22. D. W. Winnicott, 'Hate in the Counter-Transference', in D. W. Winnicott, *Collected Papers. Through Paediatrics to Psychoanalysis*, Tavistock, London 1947/1958.

23. Unlike Klein, for whom hate and love are expressions of innate capacities, Winnicott believed that 'the mother hates the baby before the baby hates the mother, and before the baby knows that mother hates him', D. W. Winnicott, *op. cit.*, 1947, p200.

24. A. Phillips, *Winnicott*, Fontana, London 1988, p89.

25. These implications are applicable across cultures. It is a matter for empirical inquiry how babies' ruthlessly narcissistic demands are expressed and contained and responded to in different times and places, how they change with time and with what effects.

26. D.W. Winnicott, *The Child, the Family and the Outside World*, Penguin, Harmondsworth 1964, p204, cited in A. Phillips, *op. cit.*, p67.

27. *Ibid.*

28. S. Frosh, 'Fathers' Ambivalence Too', in W. Hollway and B. Featherstone (eds), *Mothering and Ambivalence*, Routledge, London 1997, pp37-53.

29. This condition has been universal until now. The consequent phantasies on both sides and their effect on the relationship would be universal too, although expressed in specific ways, depending for example on dominant representations of mothers in a given culture.

30. J. Chasseguet-Smirgel, *Female Sexuality*, Virago, London 1976/1981.

31. N. Chodorow and S. Contratto, 'The Fantasy of the Perfect Mother' in N. Chodorow, *Feminism and Psychoanalytic Theory*, Yale University Press, New Haven and London 1989, p90.

32. It is important to clarify a conceptual distinction here: that between recognising a child's communications (responding to its gestures), and meeting its needs. Winnicott was interested primarily in the child's needs for recognition (a category that does not appear in Ruddick's understanding of maternal work).

33. Although 'true' is a contentious claim, I am using it intentionally, consistent with my critique of relativism. While much of the evidence for this claim derives from late modern, western cultures, it is unlikely to be lim-

ited to these. However, the mother's effectivity will be expressed differently according to cultural and social positions. See for example L. Murray, 'The Impact of Postnatal Depression on Infant Development', *Journal of Child Psychology and Psychiatry*, 33 (3) 1992, pp543-561.

34. R. Minsky, *op. cit.*, p52.

35. D.W. Winnicott, *The Family and Individual Development*, Tavistock, London 1965.

36. J. Benjamin, 'Master and Slave: The Fantasy of Erotic Domination', in A. Snitow, C. Stansell and S. Thompson (eds), *Desire: The Politics of Sexuality*, Virago, London 1984, pp301, 293. In this statement, Benjamin illustrates one good reason why psychoanalytic theory does focus on the mother-child relationship: because of the common reality. Psychoanalysis does not tend to talk about families or parents when it means mothers and this is usually because it sees the maternal relationship as distinct and unique for the child, both consciously and unconsciously. It can be argued that psychoanalysis is ideologically blinded in so doing. Alternatively, it can be argued that psychoanalytic theory is reflecting the significance of mothers in the internal and external realities of the people it tries to understand and to help.

37. See also K. Lombardi, 'Mother as Object, Mother as Subject: Implications for Psychoanalytic Developmental Theory', *Gender and Psychoanalysis* 3 (1), 1998, pp33-45.

38. B. Featherstone, *op. cit.*

39. J. Benjamin, *Shadow of the Other*, Routledge, New York and London 1998.

40. R. Minsky, *op. cit.*, p13.

41. For aspects of this debate, see J. Mens-Verheulst, K. Shreurs & L. Woertman (eds), *Daughtering and Mothering*, Routledge, London 1993; K. Lombardi, *op. cit.*; and D. Stern, *The Interpersonal World of the Infant*, Basic Books, New York 1985.

42. D.W. Winnicott, *op. cit.*, 1947; D.W. Winnicott, 'Transitional Objects and Transitional Phenomena', in D.W. Winnicott, *Collected Papers: Through Paediatrics to Psycho-Analysis*, Tavistock, London 1951/1958.

43. R. Parker, *op. cit.*, 1995, p115.

44. D.W. Winnicott, *op. cit.*, 1965, p141, quoted in E. Rayner, *The Independent Mind in British Psychoanalysis*, Free Assocation Books, London 1990, p131.

45. W.R. Bion, 'Attacks on Linking', *International Journal of Psycho-Analysis*, 40, 1959, p103, quoted in R.D. Hinshelwood, *A Dictionary of Kleinian Thought*, Free Association Books, London 1991, p247.

46. *Ibid.*

47. *Ibid.*

48. D.W. Winnicott, *Babies and their Mothers*, Free Association Books, London 1968, p90.

49. Using Kleinian principles, F. Alford regards 'the integration of love and hate' to be the common task 'faced by every human being'. F. Alford, *Melanie Klein and Critical Social Theory*, Yale University Press, New Haven and London 1989, p152.

50. R. Parker, *op. cit.*, 1995.
51. I am aware of the critiques of developmentalism (for example E. Burman, *Deconstructing Developmental Psychology*, Routledge, London 1994) and the consequent pressure to abandon the term 'development'. I prefer to retain it, but to take care not to embrace connotations of development as fixed, inevitable or teleological.
52. Britton, *op. cit.*, argues that a child's experience in a triangle, rather than a dyad, is important in this move. The third person may be the father, but significant aspects of the logic of his argument apply whether this is the case or not.
53. This bears upon the debate about an ethic of care and its relation to gender (C. Gilligan, *In a Different Voice*, Harvard University Press, Cambridge 1981; J. Tronto, *Moral Boundaries*, Routledge, London 1993; W. Hollway, 1999b 'Rethinking Moral Development for an Ethics of Care: A Kleinian Perspective on Moral Subjectivity', *Centre for Research on Family, Kinship and Childhood, Working Paper 15*, University of Leeds 1999b; S. Sevenhuijsen, *Citizenship and the Ethics of Care*, Routledge, London 1998).
54. For example, see J. Maynes and P. Best, 'In the Company of Women: Experiences of Working with the Lost Mother', in W. Hollway and B. Featherstone (eds), *Mothering and Ambivalence*, Routledge, London 1997, pp119-135.
55. B.J. Risman, 'Intimate Relationships from a Microstructural Perspective: Men who Mother,' *Gender and Society*, 1, 1987, pp6-32.
56. J. Kristeva, *The Kristeva Reader*, Trans T. Moi, Blackwell, Oxford 1992, p200, quoted in R. Minsky, *op. cit.*, p119.
57. R. Britton, *op. cit.*

Critical psychology for critical action

Isaac Prilleltensky and Stephanie Austin

Critical psychology challenges the values, assumptions, and practices of main-stream psychology. Whereas this movement offers alternatives to dominant values and assumptions, it has yet to develop a set of practices that would lead to routine critical action. Hitherto, the theoretical pole of the research-action dialectic has received more attention than its applied component. There is a need to bridge the gap between reflection and action. Otherwise, we risk irrelevancy in the cause of resisting oppression and promoting emancipation. In this paper we argue that it is not only desirable but also possible to translate the theoretical underpinnings of critical psychology into action. We apply the central values and assumptions of critical psychology to formulate recommendations for action. We propose an integrative action framework that attends to philosophical, contextual, experiential, and pragmatic considerations.

Key words: praxis, social change, interdisciplinary models, political action, theory, philosophy, oppression, emancipation

We cannot speak for all critical psychologists, nor can we hope to represent *the* critical psychology, for such a monolithic entity does not exist. What we can, and should, do is adopt a stance and explain the type of critical psychology we espouse. The critical psychology we propose is critical of the status quo in psychology because it supports forms of domination, *and* critical of the status quo in society because it perpetuates forms of oppression.[1] In our view, critical psychologists cannot help but become critical citizens as well.[2]

For us, critical psychology is about resisting oppression and promoting emancipation, it is about the lack of social justice and how psychology masks social injustice, about the lack of caring and compassion for the disadvantaged, and about psychology's indifference to social domination. As critical psychologists and critical citizens, we should strive to create a psychology that works for, and not against, the oppressed. Although various trends within critical psychology concentrate on different themes, we believe this basic tenet is common to most of them.[3] As an academic and political movement, critical psychology pursues emancipatory aims and actions. This common thread is present in German Critical Psychology, in South American Liberation Psychology, and in contemporary Western Critical Psychology.

The philosophical roots of critical psychology are intimately linked with its historical development as a political movement. German Critical Psychology emerged in the context of radical political and social movements in the 1960s and 1970s, due in large part to the work of its founder and promoter Klaus Holzkamp. Challenging the status quo in society by critiquing traditional structures and procedures was characteristic of post-war Germany.[4]

South-American Liberation Psychology followed the philosophical and historical underpinnings of Liberation Theology.[5] Liberation psychology emerged as an attempt to reinterpret mainstream psychology in light of the experiences of people who are disadvantaged. The work of Martín-Baró is important because it clearly defines an alternative to traditional formulations of psychology.[6] He proposed a psychology that explicitly concerns itself with ending oppression and promoting emancipation. In contrast to mainstream psychology, a liberation psychology is one that is historically grounded, and that does not abstract its subjects from their social and political contexts.

The emergence of community psychology in North-America has also participated in setting the stage for contemporary critical psychology in its attempt to move beyond the ahistorical, asocial, and value neutral assumptions of mainstream psychology.[7] The recognition that psychology has contributed to the exclusion of certain powerless groups in society has also been significant in the development of critical psychology. Work being done in the areas of anti-racism and feminism has played a pivotal role in the advancement of Western critical psychology.[8]

Critical discourses in the 1980s indicated a shift away from Marxism toward postmodernism. Disappointed by the failure of Marxist social utopias, many French and German postmodern philosophers moved to new ideas.[9] The advent of postmodernism, particularly in Europe, marked a recognition that the project of modernity had not been realised to an extent that would make a liberated or emancipated subjectivity possible. The way power was being reconceptualised was greatly influenced by the work of Michel Foucault.[10] Attempting to move away from dichotomous thinking to communicate the subtlety with which power operates in and through our lives, Foucault's work provides a more complex analysis. Consistent with the conceptual shift proposed by Foucault, it has been suggested that 'rather than power being equated with oppression and seen as a negative thing, which can be got rid of come the revolution, power is seen as productive, inherently neither positive nor negative: productive of knowledges, meanings and values, and of certain practices as opposed to others'.[11]

Resisting oppression, promoting emancipation

Oppression and emancipation are at the core of critical psychology. As psychologists, we can be victims of oppression or accomplices in domination. The same can be said for the citizens critical psychologists work with: they can suffer from oppression and they can engage in the oppression of others. Neither we, critical psychologists, nor the people we work with are exclusively oppressors or victims. We all have differential levels of power in the various contexts of our lives. But subjectivity and agency are not defined by oppression alone; psychologists and citizens can have an emancipatory impact; they can promote personal and collective liberation.

By oppression we mean both a state of subjugation and a process of exclusion and exploitation. Oppression involves psychological as well as political dimensions. In light of these central characteristics, Prilleltensky and Gonick define oppression as 'a state of asymmetric power relations characterised by domination, subordination, and resistance, where the dominating persons or groups exercise their power by restricting access to material resources and by implanting in the subordinated persons or groups fear or self-deprecating views about themselves'.[12] Oppression involves structural inequality which is reproduced by the everyday practices of a well-intentioned liberal citizenry. As Young clearly explains, the causes of oppression 'are embedded in unquestioned norms, habits, and symbols, in the assumptions underlying institutional rules and the collective consequences of following those rules'.[13]

When we invoke emancipation, we refer to the person's life opportunities as they relate to power.[14] Liberation involves a dialectical relationship between 'subjective experience' and 'power.' As psychologists whose central focus it is to further understand and ameliorate human experience, it is essential that we concern ourselves with power. Similar to the definition of oppression, emancipation can be conceptualised both as a state and a process which includes psychological and political dimensions. Emancipation is the experience of symmetric power relations characterised by equitable and respectful alliances between persons, communities, and nations, whereby people are free from internal and external sources of oppression and free to express and explore their physical, emotional, intellectual, and spiritual human qualities. This notion of emancipation builds on Fromm's dual conception of freedom; *freedom from* social and psychological sources of oppression, and *freedom to* pursue one's objectives in life.[15] Freedom from social oppression entails the experience of liberation from class exploitation, gender domination, and ethnic discrimination, for instance. Freedom from internal sources includes overcoming fears, obsessions, or other intra-psychic phenomena that interfere with a person's subjective experience of well-being.

The critical psychology we promote is guided by a set of values, assumptions, and practices. These parameters help to define what we mean by critical psychology and also to facilitate dialogue; they are neither perennial nor ubiquitous; they do not apply equally to different social and cultural contexts, nor are they static. In fact, they have been revised often to reflect a changing understanding of society and psychology.[16] But these limitations notwithstanding, these parameters are useful tools for deconstructing mainstream psychology and for constructing critical psychology. Table 1 shows the potentially oppressive and emancipatory impact of values, assumptions, and practices.

Values

Values guide the process of working towards a desired state of affairs; they inform our personal, professional, and political behaviour. But values are not only beneficial in that they guide behaviour towards a future outcome, for they also have inherent worth. We espouse values like empowerment, caring, and solidarity, not just because they lead towards a good or better society, but also because they have intrinsic merit as well.[17]

Table 1

The Oppressive and Emancipatory Potential of Values, Assumptions, and Practices in Psychology

	OPPRESSIVE	EMANCIPATORY
VALUES		
Personal values	When belief in agency leads to self-blame	When belief in agency leads to personal empowerment
Relational values	When participatory processes obstruct social action and mask inequality	When participatory processes afford voice and choice
Collective values	When the good of the collective comes at the expense of individual needs	When bargaining powers, resources and obligations are shared equitably
ASSUMPTIONS		
Knowledge	When used to promote only dominant ways of knowing	When used to promote subordinated ways of knowing
Good life	When success is ascribed to personal merit alone	When success is understood as a combination of personal merit and interdependence
Good society	When inequality is present	When equity is present
Power in relationships	When power differentials ignore or reproduce injustice	When power is shared and used equitably
PRACTICES		
Problem definition	When used to pathologise people	When used to give people agency
Role of client	When helping relationship promotes client passivity	When helping relationship promotes the client's active participation
Role of psychologist	When arrogates power	When shares power
Type of intervention	When focussed on intrapsychic level alone	When focussed on multiple levels of human experience (intra, inter, extra)

'Values may be defined as enduring prescriptive or proscriptive beliefs that a specific mode of conduct (instrumental value) or end state of existence (terminal value) is preferred to another mode of conduct or end state'.[18] The values of critical psychology can be classified into three groups: (a) *personal values* (e.g., self-determination, autonomy, health and personal growth), (b) *collective values* (e.g., social justice, support for community structures), and (c) *relational values* (e.g., respect for human diversity, collaboration and democratic participation). These categories reflect the need to balance individual and social goals, as well as the need for dialogue in resolving conflicts of interests. There is a dialectic between personal and collective values; one kind cannot exist without the other. While this dialectic has been amply recognized,[19] what is often missed in the literature is the need for relational values that mediate between the good of the individual and the good of the collective, a need that is often invoked in feminist and Native writings, but that is rarely discussed in mainstream social philosophy.[20] Neither personal nor collective values can exist without mechanisms for connection between them.[21]

Whether we like it or not, personal fulfilment and emancipation are linked to the contentment of the group.[22] Violent neighbourhoods and families constrain personal emancipation. Poorly-resourced communities limit opportunities for health and development. High-quality public institutions benefit the community at large.

It is often the case that personal and collective values come into conflict. Smokers demand their right to engage in the habit, public health officials uphold the public good by imposing smoking bans; employers demand more work for less pay, workers resist exploitation. Ideally, personal and collective values would be mutually enhancing, but it is often the case that conflicts arise. In order to deal with them, we should promote partnership values, values that uphold conflict resolution and collaboration without masking power differences .[23]

A delicate balance between personal and collective values is needed to promote a society in which the good of the private citizen is not inimical to the good of the society. Unless we take care to avert value excesses, we end up with conditions in which individuals are either oppressed because of totalitarian collectives or alienated from each other because of flagrant individualism. The personal and the collective are so dialectical and intertwined that one cannot flourish without the other. For that reason, we recommend thinking about the interdependence of values. To uphold *personal values*, we suggest the following:

a. Promote the ability of community members to pursue their chosen goals in life *in consideration* of other people's needs and without oppressing others,

b. Promote the physical and emotional well-being of individuals through acquisition of skills and behavioural change *in consideration* of structural and economic oppressive factors impinging on the health of the population at large,

and

c. Promote the personal growth of community members *in consideration* of vital community structures needed to advance individual health and personal emancipation.

To foster *collective values*, we suggest these ideas:

a. Promote fair allocation of bargaining powers, resources, and obligations in society *in consideration* of people's differential power, needs and abilities to express themselves, and

b. Promote vital structures that meet the needs of entire communities *in consideration* of the risks of curtailing individual freedoms and fostering conformity and uniformity.

To advance *relational values*, we propose the following:

a. Promote respect and appreciation for diverse social identities and unique oppressions *in consideration* of the need for solidarity and the risk of social fragmentation, and

b. Promote peaceful, respectful, and equitable processes of dialogue whereby citizens have meaningful input into decisions affecting their lives, *in consideration* of differential levels of power and people's ability to articulate their needs and aspirations.

Prilleltensky and Nelson suggested that advancing the well-being of oppressed groups requires actualisation of all values in a balanced way.[24] We need to remember that within a given social ecology some values appear at the foreground of our consciousness while others remain in the background. To attain the necessary balance, we must move the neglected values to the foreground. Within the present Western context, this means re-locating the value of social justice from the background to the foreground, and pushing the obsession with personal advancement from the foreground to the background.

The challenge of harmonising personal and collective interests is not trivial. How do we promote the unique identity and rights of a certain group without sacrificing solidarity with other oppressed groups? At which point do we turn our attention to other groups suffering from discrimination? How do we balance attention to processes of dialogue with outcomes of social justice? At which point do we say that we have discussed differences of opinion long enough and that now it is time for action?[25] All these questions involve values and cannot be answered in the abstract, for each unique constellation of factors requires a unique solution. We suggest looking at personal, collective, and relational values, values that Giddens recognised as vital for 'an ethics of a globalising post-traditional society'.[26] Giddens promotes these values because they imply a 'recognition of the sanctity of human life and the universal right to happiness and self-actualisation – coupled to the obligation to promote cosmopolitan solidarity and an attitude of respect'.[27]

Assumptions

Four key assumptions affecting psychological practice have to do with the explicit or implicit notions we hold concerning the good life, the good society, knowledge, and power in relationships. Conceptions of the good life are bound to influence psychologists' actions. A psychologist who values hedonistic pursuits will approve of certain clients' actions but not of others'. On the other hand, a counsellor who firmly believes in mutuality, interdependence and social responsibility will likely influence a client's actions in another direction. The implicit conceptions of the good life held by a psychologist are bound to have an impact. The impact may turn out to be oppressive or emancipatory, but in either case it is important to acknowledge the unarticulated discourse that often informs the psychologist's actions. The same applies in the case of the good society. What type of society does a psychologist wish to promote? What type of utopia does s/he have in mind?[28] One in which individualism and alienation reign, or one in which solidarity and compassion are predominant values? The impact of conceptions of the good society is typically unrecognised because a psychologist is not supposed to let her or his 'biases' play a role in her or his work, a claim that is quite indefensible.

Assumptions regarding knowledge also play a crucial role in psychology's ability to promote oppression or emancipation. Is knowledge to be used to advance the cause of the oppressed, or is it to be gathered in sterile laboratory conditions for the purpose of fostering a pure science that is not even remotely associated with social issues of importance? Worse yet, could it be that this science is used to reproduce stereotypical assumptions about certain cultural groups, or to dominate deviant populations, or to control misbehaved children in complete disregard of contextual factors? Knowledge can be used for oppressive and regressive purposes, but it can also be used for emancipatory aims. For this reason, clarity with respect to our epistemological assumptions is vital.

Conceptions of power may determine the oppressive or emancipatory course of a therapeutic, teaching, or research relationship. Ignoring power differences, undermining them, or knowingly taking advantage of them lead to abusive or disrespectful interactions. Awareness of power dynamics in relationships involving psychologists is crucial. It is only when we are aware of our power that we can begin to question its conscious or unconscious use for oppressive or emancipatory purposes. Table 1 shows some of the circumstances under which assumptions about the good life, the good society, knowledge, and power can contribute to oppression or emancipation.

Practices

Values and assumptions are manifested in practice. We concentrate on four features of practice: *problem definition, role of psychologist, role of citizen,* and *type of intervention.* Problem definition in clinical, educational, or community work has direct implications for social change or social reproduction. Analyses based on intrapsychic models reinforce the societal status quo, whereas analyses based on multilevel considerations attend also to oppressive structures. In the case of children, for instance, diagnoses are frequently given in terms of intrapsychic deficits. Rarely does the psychologist challenge institutional arrangements, however oppressive they might be.

Citizens using psychological services may be regarded as mere recipients of services or as full and active participants of the helping process. Depending on the role assigned to clients, psychologists contribute to empowerment or disempowerment. The level of participation of clients in decisions affecting their lives is affected by the value ascribed by the psychologist to democratic participation and respect for human diversity.

Psychologists may assume a highly directive role, impart expertise, or facilitate personal growth; they can act as agents of social change or social control. The choice of role is influenced by the psychologist's values and has an impact on his or her ability to be caring, to promote egalitarian relations with clients, and to foster meaningful participation of clients. An appreciation of the diverse roles psychologists need to play to resist oppression and promote emancipation is essential. Therapy and research are not enough. When disempowering social conditions curtail people's opportunities in life, a psychologist's role as a social-change agent may be called for. Community organising and political action may be the best vehicles for the promotion of human welfare in this case. One mode of helping and operating does not fit all problems.

The type of intervention chosen by a psychologist has direct implications for reproducing oppressive social structures or for changing them. A psychologist who is treating a child with behaviour problems may choose to intervene at the individual, family, school, and/or community levels. He or she may look only at the symptom or may look at the health of the child in a holistic manner. Each decision says something about the psychologist's conceptualisation of the problem and about his or her willingness to challenge oppressive structures. Table 1 summarises the potential repercussions of practices that can lead either to oppression or emancipation.

A Framework for Action
Criteria for Critical Action
Clarity with respect to values is a necessary but insufficient condition for the promotion of critical psychology praxis. Values are enacted by agents with conflicting political agendas in social contexts that are saturated with power differentials. The abstract compilation of ideal values requires immersion in complicated social settings. To enact values in specific social contexts we need to pay attention to assumptions regarding (a) *power*, (b) *legitimacy* (c) *action*, and (d) *processes*. In order to promote a balanced approach among personal, collective, and relational values, we need to engage in a balancing act with respect to each one of these four assumptions.

With respect to *power*, it is imperative that we listen to the multiple voices vying for scarce social resources and for cultural recognition. We have to balance the voices of the powerful with the voices of the oppressed. Most social policies are conceived in the absence of meaningful input from those most affected by them.[29] Exclusion is also experienced by populations controlled by psychologists: students, clients, children, or community groups.[30]

Critical assumptions about *legitimacy* require that we strike a balance between deductive and inductive approaches to knowledge and ethics, and that we complement theoretical epistemologies with grounded input. Abstract philosophical analyses of what values can lead to a good life and a good society are useful but limited.[31] What good is it to have an internally-consistent framework of values that does not reflect the living realities of most people? The corollary of this question is that *moral philosophy is not enough*. On the other hand, we can ask what is the point of knowing people's needs and aspirations if that knowledge is not processed into principles and guidelines for action? The main corollary of this question is that *grounded knowledge is not enough*.[32]

Moral philosophy and grounded experience are complementary. Theories of values have to be validated with lived experience. Otherwise, we can end up with notions that are theoretically flawless but practically useless. When proposing a set of values, it is crucial to appreciate the 'dynamic complexity and diversity of specific situations, and the particular needs, desires, intellectual and emotional habits of the persons participating in them'.[33] A framework for values should strive to answer Toulmin's call for an approach that is 'particular not universal, local not general, timely not eternal, and – above all – concrete not abstract'.[34]

Asking people what they regard as important in life is essential, but not enough to guide action. This approach is incomplete because, as an example, people can wish upon others objectionable and reprehensible things. Thus, we need philosophical critique of people's voices as much as grounded validation of conceptual frameworks.

Critical assumptions about *action* call for a balance between theory and practice. This is needed to ensure that theoretical knowledge does not remain the sole object of intellectual play. But the impetus for action should be tempered by the need to understand our own subjectivity, our political aspirations, and the risks and benefits involved in any chosen course of action. With respect to *processes*, a balance between processes and outcomes is needed to ensure that dialogue is not an end in itself. By the same token, we need to assert that ends do not justify any means.

A Model for Critical Action

Praxis refers to the unity of theory and action. This is the stage where the dialectic between conceptualisation and application gets played out. This is the moment when critical values descend from the intellectual Olympus to be debated in arenas of social contestation. This is where lived experience informs philosophy and social science, where social-change strategies complement visions of the good society, and where community members have as much sway as intellectuals.

Table 2

A Framework for Integrative Action in Critical Psychology

Considerations	Probe state of affairs	Consult	Study	Seek
Philosophical	What should be ideal vision?	Moral and political philosophers	Philosophical discourse	Vision of good life and good society
Contextual	What is actual state of affairs?	Social scientists	Economic, social, and cultural trends, as well as subjectivity	Identification of prevailing norms and social conditions
Experiential	What is missing from desirable state of affairs?	Community members	Grounded theory and lived experience	Identification of human needs
Pragmatic	What can be done to change oppressive state of affairs?	Agents of change	Resource mobilisation and social-change theory	Social-change strategies and act on them

Table 2 integrates critical psychology values and assumptions into a praxis-oriented framework. The first point to be noted is that the four sets of praxis considerations are fully complementary; praxis depends on equal attention to all of them. The framework we propose consists of *philosophical, contextual, experiential,* and *pragmatic* considerations. According to table 2, each set of considerations calls on the critical psychologist to probe various states of affairs, to consult multiple voices, to research different sources, and to seek various and complementary outcomes. The unique contribution of the framework is that it integrates praxis considerations that have hitherto been studied in isolation. Whereas some critical psychologists concentrate on contextual configurations of power and discourse, others explore needs and experiences of a particular population, and still a third group focuses on social change.[35] This framework integrates the various strands of critical psychology into a praxis-oriented model. The model incorporates multiple voices, combines research and action, draws on various disciplines, pays attention to power and contextual considerations, and can be applied to guide and examine critical psychology practice.

The reason we need four sets of considerations is that each one by itself is insufficient to cover the ground necessary for praxis. *Philosophical considerations* are needed to evaluate the merits and drawbacks of diverse scenarios of the good life and the good society. Moral and political philosophers examine potential contradictions among competing ideals and spend considerable time formulating coherent visions. Philosophers contribute to praxis by debating the ideal vision we should strive for.

Our implicit and explicit notions of what constitutes the good life and the good society are going to have an impact on the interventions and programmes we develop for people who come into contact with psychologists. But convincing philosophical positions notwithstanding, they are insufficient to mount social policies that meet human needs. An ever-present danger in philosophical discourse is its detachment from the social conditions in which people live. To counteract this risk we need to explore the contextual circumstances that complement philosophical considerations.

Contextual considerations explore what is the actual state of affairs in which people live. Social scientists strive to understand what are the social, economic, cultural, and political conditions of a specific community. This line of inquiry helps us to determine social norms and cultural trends influencing people's choices, discourses, and behaviour. A contextual assessment is necessary to understand the subjective experience of residents of a particular community. Individualist and collectivist societies differ markedly with respect to socialisation, customs, and visions of the good society. Poor and rich communities vary with regard to the importance they ascribe to basic necessities.

Values attain their meaning within a social context. The meaning of self-determination in an individualist society is vastly different from its connotation in a collectivist environment. In a totally collectivist society, citizens yearn for more autonomy and resent state and communal intrusion. Examples include 'curtailing individual rights in the name of community needs; suppressing creativity in the name of conformity; and even suppressing a sense of self, losing individuality in a mesh of familial or communal relations'.[36] In an individualist environment, on the other hand, citizens wish to experience more sense of community and less selfishness.

We understand values more fully when we comprehend the set of circumstances within which they are embedded.[37] Pushed to extremes, values lose their merit. Excessive collectivism violates one's right to privacy, while flagrant individualism numbs our sensitivity to others and leads to desolation. It is incumbent upon us, then, to watch out for signs of value immoderation.[38] The moment one principle takes too much space, others shrink proportionately. Applied to North American society, this means that collectivist values such as solidarity, sharing, co-operation, and social justice have shrunk in reverse proportion to the increase in individualism.[39]

Experiential considerations infuse philosophical and contextual considerations with human needs and sentiments. It is not enough for philosophers to ponder what the rest of us need, or for social scientists to recommend what will make our communities a better place to live. Philosophical tenets have to be validated with the lived experience of community members and with the knowledge of social scientists.[40] It is only when most people attest to the benefits of having voice and choice that the abstract notion of self-determination becomes meaningful.

The consideration of needs contributes to praxis by answering the question: what is missing? and what is a desirable state of affairs for community members? This set of considerations pays explicit attention to the voice of the people with whom we partner to reduce oppressive conditions. Qualitative methods, grounded theory, and lived experience serve to identify basic human needs of people in the particular contexts of their lives.

Whereas the previous sets of considerations examined actual, ideal, and desirable states of affairs, *pragmatic considerations* concern feasible social change. Unlike previous deliberations, which asked what is, what is missing, or what should be, the main question answered by this set of considerations is what can be done. This question is meant to bridge the gap between the actual state of affairs on one hand, and desirable and ideal visions on the other. Feasible change draws our attention to what social improvements can be realistically accomplished – a distinct political goal. A specific outcome of pragmatic thinking is a plan for social action.

The complementary nature of the four sets of considerations now becomes apparent: without a philosophical analysis we lack a vision; without a contextual analysis we lack an understanding of social forces; without a needs-assessment we lack an idea of what people want; and finally, without pragmatic thinking we lack a plan of action. The interdependence of these deliberations makes it impossible to privilege one set of considerations over another.

Opportunities for action: two case studies

The challenge now is to translate critical psychology values, assumptions and models of praxis into concrete applications. In this section, we will describe two examples of action-oriented research projects that illustrate how the conceptual tools we have outlined in this paper have been useful in applied critical work. The praxis framework can be used to evaluate current social policy debates and to guide critical psychology research and action. Isaac is part of a team of researchers who received a grant from a federal agency to write a book on the promotion of family wellness and the prevention of child maltreatment. The team's work followed the four praxis considerations delineated in the article. The research design included philosophical, contextual, experiential, and pragmatic considerations. The first section of the report we wrote deals extensively with a vision and values for child and family wellness. We based the vision for wellness on philosophical writings, and on extensive consultations with a wide range of stakeholders, including youth, parents, child welfare workers, researchers, administrators and policy makers. All of these stakeholder groups had a chance to express their vision for child and family wellness. In doing so, we met the criteria for merging philosophical with grounded input, but the deliberations within our own research team were not without controversy. Whereas some team members wanted to be quite vocal about the need to address social injustice in child wellness, others preferred a more cautious approach that refrained from controversial political statements. Our team re-enacted familiar debates within the social sciences, with some colleagues in favour of being very explicit about our own value-base, and others reluctant to come across as too radical. Interestingly enough, the community psychologists within our group were more comfortable with explicit value statements, whereas those from other disciplines were apprehensive about such edicts. This conflict necessitated a fair amount of discussion and negotiation among the various sides.

Our report also dealt extensively with the context for the promotion of wellness and the prevention of abuse. As in the previous section, our writing was based on a very thorough review of empirical research and on original qualitative interviews and focus groups with more than 130 stakeholders. The same consultation process was used to ask the various key informant groups about the needs of children and families in general, and of those at-risk in particular. Thus, our participants had a chance to articulate the needs of the population of interest. This exercise followed the praxis framework in that it facilitated the merging of expert and professional opinions with those of the people experiencing the problems themselves.

Sensitive to the contextual considerations of child and family wellness, our team had two researchers exploring these issues in aboriginal communities. These two team members, one of them of aboriginal ancestry, and the other very experienced in work with native communities, studied in depth the cultural, sociological, and psychological dynamics of child wellness and child abuse in native communities. Their work culminated in the longest chapter of our book, devoted to child wellness in the context of aboriginal families and communities.

To complete the cycle of praxis, members of our team realised that we needed to go beyond documenting promising programmes and policies. In addition to preparing accessible summary bulletins documenting the main findings and distributing those widely across the country, Canada in this case, a few of us formed a child advocacy group designed to lobby on behalf of children. We used our findings to demand from government more action on child and family wellness. The group, called Action for Children, is a coalition of parents, child professionals, physicians, academics, and community members. Some of our social action initiatives took place in the context of an upcoming election. They included (a) writing a petition demanding that all politicians commit themselves to a series of initiatives to improve child and family wellness, (b) organising a letter-writing campaign to local newspapers to draw attention to the plight of children at risk, (c) distributing informational brochures in the community, and (d) publishing large ads in newspapers calling on the public to vote in the election for a party that would pay serious attention to children's issues. The group also made formal presentations to a government task-force dealing with young children, and some of our members attended presentations by politicians and questioned them about government action on behalf of children.

A tangible achievement of the family wellness project was a collaboration with the local United Way that resulted in a commitment of the agency to increase its funding for primary prevention from 4 per cent of their annual budget to 10 per cent. This is in addition to a long-term commitment in principle to eliminate child abuse in the region. Such commitment has already influenced resource allocations and has been assumed as a priority by the governing board. This collaboration responds to the action component of the praxis framework. There are many research projects that end up on shelves. Guided by the call for action, we ventured into the community, disseminated our findings widely, and made sure people used them.

Similarly, I (Stephanie) was involved in the creation and implementation of an action-research project that reflected philosophical, contextual, experiential and pragmatic considerations. As students in a Women and Health course in the winter of 1995, three of us met and decided we wanted to develop a community-based prevention project in response to what we were learning in class. Our inspiration to act came from our academic exposure to various feminist theories and empirical studies on the decline in young women's health during early adolescence. We were learning about young women's loss of self-confidence, their difficulties with body image, their low levels of participation in physical activities, the increasing rates of drop-out in the sciences, and other such indicators of poor mental and physical health.

In collaboration and consultation with young women, other community organisations and academics, we started a programme called POWER Camp (Partnerships On Women's Educational Realities) that caters specifically to the needs of girls eleven – fifteen years. The programme is committed to: a) fostering a positive self-image among its participants; b) increasing young women's awareness through diverse experiences; c) creating opportunities for girls to become advocates of their own lives; and d) providing individuals and groups within the community opportunities to critically explore means of creative and active living. POWER Camp is about a holistic approach to young women's empowerment. In order to create an environment in which young women can be empowered, POWER Camp has become 'a place where women come together when life tries to tear them apart. It's a result of listening'.[41] The focus is on girls' capacities, not their deficiencies.

Together with campers, women from the community and facilitators, we create a learning environment at POWER Camp which is designed to touch not only upon philosophical knowledge, but also upon contextually determined attitudes, values and ways of being, and upon know-how. We are committed to creating an environment in which young women can listen to one another and be listened to, can respectfully challenge one another and be challenged, and can support one another and be supported. POWER Camp's programming is based on a progression from personal exploration and self-understanding, to actively engaging in community-based projects that transform the social, political, economic and physical environments in which we all live. The themes of each two-week session are: creative self-expression, the earth and our bodies, active living, and activism. As the programming illustrates, we are not only concerned with young women's personal self-perceptions, but also with societal knowledge regarding what it means to be a young woman in this social context. POWER Camp is responsive to the diverse needs and backgrounds of young women, demonstrating by example how we can all contribute to the creation of pro-feminist, anti-racist and inclusive social settings.

Another action-oriented outcome that stems from this work is that it creates a forum through which young women coming out of university can put their feminist theory to practice, using their knowledge and skills to create their own employment. As an alternative feminist organisation, POWER Camp was established in response to a gap in the services available to young women. In so doing, POWER Camp also accomplishes an important role in social transformation. With the hope of creating a multiplying effect within the community, POWER Camp services include workshops in schools with adolescent girls and with mixed-gender groups in addition to the two-week long summer day-camp sessions for young women. In an effort to share the 'how' of our work with other interested groups, POWER Camp also offers workshops at conferences and for community organisations.

As an organisation and as an educational initiative, we make political links between all forms of systemic discrimination (i.e., sexism, racism, classism, ableism, ageism, etc.). POWER Camp emphasises the often-overlooked importance of working for significant and lasting social changes through a redefinition of policies and practices at the institutional level. We have therefore been involved in numerous initiatives aimed at altering policies related to youth, women, education, health and social services.

Conclusion

Critical psychology requires a praxis orientation as much as mainstream psychology requires a critical psychology. To promote the dialectic between discourse and action, we offered three sets of conceptual tools: values, assumptions, and considerations related to praxis. These are tools and not solutions. They may be used as a compass, not a map. Each concrete challenge, embedded in a specific context, requires a unique combination of values, assumptions and practices, and entails a new solution every time.

Earlier versions of this paper were presented at the Millennium World Conference in Critical Psychology in Sydney, Australia, April, 1999; and at the Inter-American Congress of Psychology in Caracas, Venezuela, June, 1999.

Notes

1. I. Prilleltensky, *The Morals and Politics of Psychology: Psychological Discourse and the Status Quo*, State University of New York Press, Albany, NY 1994; I. Prilleltensky, 'Bridging Agency, Theory, and Action: Critical links in Critical Psychology', in T. Sloan (ed), *Voices in Critical Psychology*, Macmillan, London in press.
2. S. Reicher, 'Laying the Ground for a Common Critical Psychology', in T. Ibáñez and L. Íñiguez (eds), *Critical Social Psychology*, Sage, London 1997, pp83-94.
3. See for example B.M. Braginsky and D.D. Braginsky, *Mainstream Psychology: A Critique*, Holt, Rinehart, and Winston, New York 1974; D. Fox and I. Prilleltensky (eds), *Critical Psychology: An Introduction*, Sage, London 1997; T. Ibáñez and L. Íñiguez (eds), *Critical Social Psychology*, Sage, London 1997; I. Martin-Baró, *Writings for a Liberation Psychology*, Harvard University Press, Cambridge, MA 1994; I. Parker and R. Spears

(eds), *Psychology and Society*, Pluto Press, Chicago 1996; E. V. Sullivan, *A Critical Psychology*, Plenum, New York 1984; T. Teo, 'Prolegomenon to a Contemporary Psychology of Liberation', *Theory and Psychology*, 8(4), 1998b, pp527-547; T. Teo, 'Methodologies of Critical Psychology: Illustrations From the Field of Racism', *Annual Review of Critical Psychology*; C.W. Tolman, *Psychology, Society, and Subjectivity: An Introduction to German Critical Psychology*. Routledge, London 1994.

4. T. Teo, 'Klaus Holzkamp and the Rise and Decline of German Critical Psychology', *History of Psychology*, 1(3), 1998a, pp235-253; C.W. Tolman and W. Maiers (eds), *Critical Psychology: Contributions to an Historical Science of the Subject*, Cambridge University Press, New York 1991.

5. P. Berryman, *Liberation Theology: The Essential Facts About the Revolutionary Movement in Latin America and Beyond*, Pantheon Books, New York, New York 1987, p87.

6. I. Martin-Baró, *op. cit.*

7. S.B. Sarason, *Psychology Misdirected*, The Free Press, New York, NY 1981; E.E. Sampson, *Justice and the Critique of Pure Psychology*, Plenum Press, New York, NY 1983.

8. For work done in these two areas see for example F. M. Moghaddam and C. Studer, 'Cross-Cultural Psychology: The Frustrated Gadfly's Promises, Potentialities, and Failures', in D. Fox and I. Prilleltensky (eds), *Critical Psychology: An Introduction*, Sage Publications, Thousand Oaks, CA 1997, pp185-201; T. Teo, *op. cit.*, in press; E. Burman (ed), *Feminists and Psychological Practice*, Sage, London 1990; A. Mulvey, 'Community psychology and feminism: tensions and commonalities', *Journal of Community Psychology*, 16, 1988, p70; S. Wilkinson, 'Feminist Psychology', in D. Fox & I. Prilleltensky (eds), *Critical Psychology: An Introduction*, Sage, London 1997, pp247-264.

9. T. Teo, 'Practical Reason in Psychology: Postmodern Discourse and a Neo-modern Alternative', in C. W. Tolman, F. Cherry, R. van Hezewijk, and I. Lubek (eds), *Problems of Theoretical Psychology*, Captus, Toronto, ON 1996, pp280-290.

10. M. Foucault, in P. Rabinow (ed), *The Foucault Reader*, Pantheon Books, New York, NY 1984.

11. J. Henriques, W. Hollway, C. Urwin, C. Venn & V. Walkerdine, *Changing the Subject: Psychology, Social Regulation and Subjectivity*, Methuen & Co, New York, NY 1984, p237.

12. I. Prilleltensky and L. Gonick, 'Polities Change, Oppression Remains: On the Psychology and Politics of Oppression', *Political Psychology*, 17, 1996, p129.

13. I. M. Young, *Justice and the Politics of Difference*, Princeton University Press, New Jersey 1990.

14. T. Teo, *op. cit.*, 1998b.

15. E. Fromm, *Escape from Freedom*, Avon Books, New York 1965.

16. I. Prilleltensky, *op. cit.*, 1994; I. Prilleltensky, 'Values, Assumptions, and

Practices: Assessing the Moral Implications of Psychological Discourse and Action', *American Psychologist*, 47, 1997, pp517-535.

17. P. Hill Collins, 'Black Feminist Thought in the Matrix of Domination', in C. Lemert (ed), *Social Theory: The Multicultural and Classic Readings*, Westview, San Francisco 1993, pp615-626; R. Kane, *Through the Moral Maze: Searching for Absolute Values in a Pluralistic World*, Paragon, New York 1994; J. Kekes, *The Morality of Pluralism*, Princeton University Press, Princeton, NJ 1993.

18. D. M. Mayton, S. J. Ball-Rokeach & W. E. Loges, 'Human Values and Social Issues: An Introduction', *Journal of Social Issues*, 50(4), 1994, p3.

19. e.g. Z. Bauman, *Postmodern Ethics*, Blackwell, Cambridge, MA 1993; A. Melucci, *The Playing Self*, Cambridge University Press, New York, NY 1996a; A. Melucci, *Challenging Codes: Collective Action in the Information Age*, Cambridge University Press, New York, NY 1996b; M. Sandel, *Democracy's Discontent*, Harvard University Press, Cambridge, MA 1996.

20. On feminist writing see, for example, E. Frazer and N. Lacey, *The Politics of Community: A Feminist Critique of the Liberal-Communitarian Debate*, University of Toronto Press, Toronto 1993; A. Hernández, *Pedagogy, democracy, and feminism: rethinking the public sphere*, State University of New York Press, Albany, NY 1997; P. Hill Collins, *op. cit.*; A. Lorde, 'The Master's Tools will Never Dismantle the Master's House', in C. Lemert (ed), *Social Theory: The Multicultural and Classic Readings*, Westview, San Francisco 1993, pp485-487. For Native writing see, for example, P. Gunn Allen, 'Who is your Mother? Red Roots of White Feminism', in C. Lemert (ed), *Social Theory: The Multicultural and Classic Readings*, Westview, San Francisco 1993, pp649-656.

21. J. Habermas, *Moral Consciousness and Communicative Action*, MIT Press, Cambridge, MA 1990; R. W. Putnam, 'Creating Reflective Dialogue', in S. Toulmin & B. Gustavsen (eds), *Beyond Theory: Changing Organisations Through Participation*, John Benjamins North America, Philadelphia, PA 1996, pp41-52.

22. A. Melucci, *op. cit.*, 1996b.

23. G. Nelson, I. Prilleltensky & H. McGillivary, 'Value-based Partnerships: Toward Solidarity with Oppressed Groups', *American Journal of Community Psychology*, in press; R. W. Putnam, *op. cit.*, 1996.

24. I. Prilleltensky and G. Nelson, 'Community Psychology: Reclaiming Social Justice', in D. Fox & I. Prilleltensky (eds), *Critical Psychology: An Introduction*, Sage, London 1997, pp166-184.

25. S. Benhabib, 'From Identity Politics to Social Feminism: A Plea for the Nineties', in D. Trend (ed), *Radical Democracy: Identity, Citizenship, and the State*, Routledge, New York 1996, pp27-41; A. L. Jaggar, 'Introduction: Living with Contradictions', in A.L. Jaggar (ed), *Living with Contradictions: Controversies in Feminist and Social Ethics*, Westview Press, San Francisco 1994, pp1-12.

26. A. Giddens, *Beyond Left and Right: The Future of Radical Politics*, Stanford

University Press, Stanford, CA 1994, p253.

27. *Ibid.*
28. M. Michael, 'Pick a Utopia, any Utopia', in I. Parker and R. Spears (eds), *Psychology and Society: Radical Theory and Practice*, Pluto Press, Chicago 1996, pp141-152.
29. D. Taylor (ed), *Critical Social Policy*, Sage London 1996; B. Wharf and B. McKenzie, *Connecting Policy to Practice in the Human Services*, Oxford University Press, Toronto 1998.
30. E. Burman, G. Aitken, P. Alldred, R. Allwood, T. Billington, B. Goldberg, A. J. Gordo Lopez, C. Hennan, D. Marks and S. Warner, *Psychology Discourse Practice: From Regulation to Resistance*, Taylor & Francis, London, UK 1996.
31. A.L. Jaggar, *op. cit.*
32. R. Kane, 'Dimensions of Value and the Aims of Social Inquiry', *American Behavioural Scientist*, 41, 1998, pp578-597.
33. P. Bowden, *Caring: Gender-Sensitive Ethics*, Routledge, London 1997, p3.
34. S. Toulmin, 'Introduction', in S. Toulmin and B. Gustavsen (eds), *Beyond Theory: Changing Organisations Through Participation*, John Benjamins North America, Philadelphia, PA 1996, pp1-7.
35. E. Burman *et al.*, op. cit.; I. Parker and R. Spears, *op. cit.*; Teo, op. cit., in press.
36. A. Etzioni, *The New Golden Rule*, Basic Books, New York 1996, p26.
37. D. Bell, *Communitarianism and its Critics*, Clarendon Press, Oxford 1993; Etzioni, *op. cit.*, 1996.
38. R. Kane, *op. cit.*, 1994.
39. J.R. Saul, *The Unconscious Civilization*, Anansi, Concord, Ontario 1995.
40. R. Kane, *op. cit.*, 1998; M. Montero, 'Dialectic Between Active Minorities and Majorities: A Study of Social Influence in the Community', *Journal of Community Psychology*, 26, 1998, pp281-289.
41. 11-year-old POWER camper, July 1997.

Employee assistance programmes (EAPs):
From crisis support to sanctioned coercion and panopticist practices?

Margaret H. Vickers and
Alexander Kouzmin

Employee Assistance Programmes (EAPs) have been developed to provide support for organisational actors in 'trouble'. In many instances, they provide a valuable service to the 'troubled worker' who may be experiencing personal grief, work conflicts, financial problems or relationship difficulties. The evolution of EAPs and their philosophy is explored in order to expose some of the 'propaganda' that surrounds their use. 'Hank's' case, and its place as an EAP 'success story', is examined in light of the authors' views that EAPs provide possibilities for covert coercion and surveillance. The EAP process is critically considered in terms of the problematic nature of 'favoured ways of thinking', especially given the imperative of supervisory 'observation' and subsequent coercive referrals for the 'recalcitrant', 'intractable' or 'depressed' organisational member. The paper concludes with a recap on the problem of using EAPs as crisis support, sanctioned coercion or panopticist possibilities, with some pointers for future research and a critical review of the widening organisational problematic of surveillance and control.

Beware the 'propaganda'

Our society is not one of spectacle, but of surveillance; under the surface of images, one invests bodies in depth; behind the great abstraction of exchange, there continues the meticulous, concrete training of useful forces; the circuits of communication are the supports of an accumulation and a centralisation of knowledge; the play of signs defines the anchorages of power; it is not that the beautiful totality of the individual is amputated, repressed, altered by our social order, but rather that the individual is carefully fabricated in it, according to a whole technique of forces and bodies.[1]

The literature on Employee Assistance Programmes (EAPs) mostly depicts an evolving 'success story' of programmes developed by supposedly humanitarian organisations concerned for their staff. EAPs have, so the story goes, become part of the infrastructure and bloodstream of organisations through concern for the organisation's most precious commodity – their human resources – in a genuine and proactive developmental manner.[2] One needs to beware the propaganda. In the first instance, the use of the word 'commodity' alerts one to the instrumental orientations of EAPs. One needs to critically reflect upon the coercive and paternalistic realities of EAPS, and the possibilities for their continuing use as endorsed means of surveillance and social control. This is especially important as one reflects on the increasing emphasis on efficiency in modern organisations and the fundamental tension that remains between demands for efficiency and the exposure of actors to organisational trauma, especially when EAPs may not provide the humanistic panacea that is claimed.

When considering EAPs, one is reminded of the human relations school, where there also existed an outward appearance of concern for employees. Those familiar will know that human relations is very much in disgrace, at least in the West.[3] Attention was directed towards workplaces being organisations, rather than factories.[4] Managerial practices shifted away from Tayloristic disciplines to the recognition of the need to accommodate worker psychological needs. A key feature of the human relations approach was the social-engineering role given to management through maintaining equilibrium and integrating the parts of the organisation. The vehicle, in this case, was not formal structures of co-ordination and command but values, informal practices and the 'logic of sentiment'.[5] The human relations tradition, with its emphasis on social needs, provided the basis for the earliest psychological interventions.[6] One is reminded of the famous, if flawed, Hawthorne studies. The work coming out of the Hawthorne

Experiments was generally oriented towards understanding how to manipulate the behaviour of workers in order to further organisational purposes.[7] Output was a central concern and it was found that whenever any 'pessimistic' preoccupations emerged, for any reason, there was an adverse effect on output.[8] On one hand, management could take a more complete and sympathetic view of the worker. On the other, more of the worker became known to management. The possibility of workers being patronised and manipulated increased.[9]

The managerialist underpinnings of the early human relations era cannot and should not be forgotten. Human relationists have been widely criticised for their managerial bias, and for the denial of underlying economic conflicts of interest in the workplace.[10] The so-called concern for the individual did not replace the emphasis on efficiency and rationality, but became an instrument of it. One should not forget the criticisms that have been levelled at the human relationists. Similar propaganda has emerged surrounding EAPs. A critique is well overdue.

EAPs and the 'troubled worker'

It seems useful to appreciate the 'roots' of EAPs in order to enjoy a richer understanding of them – even if what is revealed is not always positive.[11] EAPs ostensibly were developed to provide support for organisational actors in 'trouble'. In many instances, they still provide a valuable service to staff experiencing personal grief, work conflicts, financial problems or relationship difficulties, providing counselling and referral services for a wide range of personal problems.[12] They also provide training for supervisors to recognise and deal with 'troubled' employees,[13] providing job-based programmes designed to *identify* and assist the troubled worker.[14] EAPs may be referred to in different ways and comprise different aspects: providing a 'performance profile'; as a work-based programme or 'job-based' programme; as an 'Employee Assistance Service' (EAS); or, as offshoots of EAPs, as 'Member Assisted Programmes' (MAPS) and, with some concern, as 'Employee *Enhancement* Programmes' (EEPs).[15] The 'troubled worker'[16] may reflect the 'problem' through tardiness, absenteeism or hostility[17] or through other, less 'discussible', behaviour – sexual misconduct, violence, drug abuse, sabotage. There are many problematic outcomes of 'observing' and 'identifying' the troubled worker. For example, marginal performers are described as *supervisory problems* – the so-called 'problem employee'.[18]

EAPs have evolved over many decades. The common use of alcohol as a mainstay in the workplace during the first half of the nineteenth century provided the grounding for the first job-based programmes, with expressions of concern about alcohol use on-the-job. Problem drinking was first intensively addressed during the 1880s, through to the 1920s, in order to organise a dependable workforce.[19] The temperance movement was reinforced by the rise of commercial efficiency during the turn-of-the-century industrialisation. Some EAP intervention was first evident in the 1930s and 1940s through a further recognition of the problems of alcoholism in the workplace.[20] EAP history is intertwined closely with that of AA, with some arguing that the EAP movement began, perhaps amateurishly, with one recovering alcoholic sharing his/her personal recovery with another.[21] It was during the late 1930s and during the war years that the rapid rise of AA, the sudden and enlarged need for workers during the war, and concern by industrial physicians, served as impetus for early programmes. However, it was during the late 1940s and early 1950s that a more discernible coherence in efforts to develop job-based alcoholism programmes emerged.[22] Even as recently as the 1970s, the initial goal for many EAPs remained linked to the identification and assistance of employees with alcohol problems.[23]

Over the ensuing decades, the focus shifted from alcohol abuse to other drugs, with EAPs increasing in visibility through the 1970s and holding, as the main aim, that worker-productivity remain unaffected.[24] EAPs have continued to be used to offer help to substance abusers but have, more recently, developed into a far broader range of services that extend far beyond issues associated with substance abuse.[25]

The instrumental philosophy behind the development of job-based programmes has traditionally been that personal problems affect job performance.[26] The tenet of the EAP movement is that employees' job performance is decreased by their psychic pain and personal troubles, which tend to be viewed as an impediment to be eliminated or brought under the control of management.[27] EAPs have been focused purely on 'job performance', and the supervisory role had responsibility for ensuring that this instrumental focus was maintained.[28] More specifically, the rationale for EAPs has been documented as being able to reduce costs; rehabilitate and retain the troubled employee; enhance management and labour relations; provide a benefit to employees and families that returns more than it costs; and to project a 'caring' image, both internally and externally.[29] Moreover, the provision of EAPs may, arguably, allow executives to employ the defence posturing of 'rationalisation',[30] allowing managers to justify to themselves (and to others) that the continuing barrage of injury that they may be responsible for (directly or indirectly) is being neatly, conveniently and humanely dealt with by the organisation. EAPs can provide an adequate, if not proper, organisational response.

One must not be blinkered by the humanistic rhetoric surrounding EAPs. EAPs are based on formal policy statements[31] and have become a lucrative, money-making venture – one of the latest 'growth industries'. They continue to grow in popularity.[32] There is a real 'boom' in EAP provider services as EAPs are used to support organisations against legislative shifts.[33] The Australian Federal *Disability Discrimination Act* (1992) (DDA) and the New South Wales *Occupational Health and Safety Act* provide examples.[34] Whilst EAPs commenced as a means to offer help to substance abusers, company-related problems associated with drug use are not merely about managerial concerns over increased accidents, violence and poor productivity. Insurance claims and, consequently, insurance premiums may be reduced for companies that adhere to a drug-free workplace programme. In many cases there is a zero tolerance for drugs: if there is an accident involving an injury and the actor tests positive for drug use, the company will lose some, if not all, of their workers' compensation rights.[35] Criminal sanctions may be imposed on employers who breach the provisions of these legislative imperatives, given their duty of care.[36] Indeed, it has been argued that the primary purpose of such support services is to minimise wrongful dismissal suits.[37] Thus, EAPs provide organisations with a programme that potentially may reduce insurance premiums, workplace accidents and lawsuits whilst also increasing worker productivity.

EAPs appear to have a bright future, although they are unlikely to mirror what they have been over the past twenty years.[38] They are now associated with drug-free workplace initiatives; disability legislation; equal employment opportunity (EEO); workplace violence;[39] risk management; critical incident debriefing; crisis management services; disability management; childcare and eldercare services; stress; HIV counselling;[40] and the support of staff enduring grief and loss.[41] Currently, the most popular model of provision of EAP services is an external provider at an external location,[42] although various combinations may exist of internal or external provider services being located either on- or off-site for the employer-client.

The propaganda surrounding EAPs is conveniently supported by euphemism. For example, the EAP catch-cry is 'people help people'.[43] One organisation named a 'committee of concern' to formulate policy designed to 'help' people and maintain a preventative focus.[44] Some organisations, such as IBM, are so enamoured of their programmes that they regard them as not being merely an EAP – they are *more* than an EAP![45] However, EAPs have also invoked 'the new paternalism', although this new paternalism is proffered as a 'necessity'.[46] The Industrial Betterment Movement sought to promote job performance through paternalism – a 'helping hand' provided because it made good business sense.[47] One sees that, more recently, some very *personal* services are also being offered to employees that seem, possibly, to be beyond the workplace scope, such as advice on infertility, child care and adoption.[48]

Emener asserts that one's task as an administrator, manager, supervisor and human resource development specialist in EAPs is to assure that employees experience an 'internalised desire to develop and grow to their fullest, and to help them feel good about themselves when they sense that there may be ways that they could improve themselves'.[49] Whilst it is acknowledged that supervisors may take pride and satisfaction from their coaching, resulting in their charges' increased maturity, the paternalistic overtones are demonstrable.[50] It must be remembered that the primary objective of EAPs is unequivocally instrumental: to return staff-members to maximum utility; to return them to work with the least fuss possible and the least productive time lost to the organisation; to save litigation; and to support public relations exercises. These objectives may be couched in more chivalrous terms, but this is the essence.

The literature demonstrates that there remain numerous unresolved questions about EAP use. For example, an actor may be observed to have a personal problem but demonstrate no deterioration in work productivity, as might be the case with a battered spouse.[51] The question of employer intervention is a sensitive one. Workers' personal problems may manifest in changes in personal behaviour rather than work performance.[52] Further, the continuing abuse of drugs and other substances in a way that affects the workplace requires employers to think carefully about the need to balance employee privacy with the organisational needs of safety and productivity, although it seems unresolved how one might do this effectively.[53] Additionally, there are conflicts in the literature about EAPs, for example, the ideological conflict between social control through performance orientation, and humanitarianism.[54] This particular cleavage extends as one contemplates the return to paternalism as a perceived means to support staff.[55] Finally, one should be aware that there has been insufficient research on *how* the troubled worker should be identified.[56]

The EAP process:
Crisis support, coercive tool or instrument of surveillance?

'Hank': An EAP 'Success' Story

Hank's case is extracted from McClure and Werther's exposition of the use of an EAP programme to successfully circumvent a potentially violent workplace incident.[57] Hank was a man who had worked for thirty years for the same company and had recently experienced what he described as 'being demoted'.[58] A new manager was appointed, who reported to Hank's previous Manager. Hank then reported to the new manager. This effectively added another level between Hank and the senior manager.

Hank felt he was being 'pushed around', and indicated 'how little the top guys appreciate what I've done for the company'.[59] Unfortunately, Hank was also a gun enthusiast who enjoyed target practice. From the report given, it seemed that the net effect of his recreational preferences, combined with an 'unsuitable' workplace attitude, resulted in a consultant recommending managerialist and panopticist 'solutions' in an effort to prevent a 'predicted' violent incident from occurring. As a result, Hank's new manager worked with the Human Resource Department and the EAP professionals to establish the requirement that Hank get a psychological assessment. It was decided that the new manager (the original source of Hank's irritation) should 'monitor' Hank's work performance and document all his behaviours – 'positive' and 'negative'. One of the reported objectives of these initiatives would be to establish that the firm had legitimate grounds for documenting and recommending his need for therapy and possible subsequent discharge from his place of employment.[60] Fortunately for Hank, and ostensibly as a result of these 'interventions', his work behaviours gradually 'improved': 'His new manager reported that Hank is not as enthusiastic as the manager would like, but that he does speak up at staff meetings and initiates more activity than in the past ... and generally deals more pleasantly with the manager'.[61] Hank was being watched by his new manager. Much of his behaviour, for example at meetings, was being monitored without his necessarily being aware. He was, as Bentham's panopticon depicts, one of the watched, where the watched don't know they are being watched.

The EAP process

There are, of course, numerous potential situations where the use of EAPs may provide a tremendous opportunity for support for organisational actors: redundancy; organisational restructures; downsizing; re-engineering; outsourcing; illness and disability in the workplace; discrimination practices; role conflict and ambiguity; stress; exposure to death in the workplace; workplace violence; and pathological management practices. All these examples demonstrate the breathtaking array of potentially traumatising events which organisational actors face. With all the potential sources of trauma associated with organisational life, there is a need for institutional support.[62] It is recognised that, under many circumstances, confidential and accessible support via counselling or other referrals may provide a vital service to staff traumatised and in need of assistance.

One role of EAPs commonly sought by employers is that of human resource (HR) or managerial consultation, such as was sought in Hank's case.[63] EAP providers are also frequently called upon to train management in *observing* the 'troubled worker', a task that has elsewhere been underscored as problematic.[64] Training of HR and other management staff may be in the areas of understanding the 'troubled employee'; motivating others to seek help; recognising problems that may exist; documenting unsatisfactory work; and successfully interviewing employees.[65]

However, the most widely-known categories of EAP usage are staff referrals. These may be, broadly, self-referrals, or supervisory or union referrals.[66] Whilst programmes may vary in their overt emphasis on self-referral, most provide for supervisory referral of staff whose performance is perceived to be impaired.[67] Certainly, self-referrals enable staff to seek confidential advice or assistance through that provider. Further, benign supervisory intervention may also be possible in the form of a gentle 'invitation' or reminder about the EAP for those staff known to be experiencing problems. The element of free choice on the part of the staff member to utilise these services (and not have others know of their choice) becomes crucial to a support service that is not coercive.

It is the supervisory referrals – 'coercive referrals'[68] – which provide an entirely different series of problematic potentialities. These potential difficulties are rarely highlighted in the 'propagandist' literature that regularly reports on EAP usage and 'success'. 'Coercive referrals' may be made by supervisors in an organisation who finds themselves dealing with what might be termed, for any number of reasons, a 'problem individual'. EAPs, in this context, focus on the marginal employee.[69] Trice and Beyer outline the strategy of 'constructive confrontation' used to counteract the denial 'tactics' used by, for example, alcoholics.[70] These kinds of special actions, taken on the part of the employer, constitute what has been termed in the personnel management and industrial relations literature, 'positive discipline'.[71] One sees that supervisors are at liberty to 'encourage' the troublesome actor to get involved with EAP services. However, failure on the part of that individual to seek help in such a situation can lead to termination.[72]

Some employers have indicated that they will be supportive of a 'problem' employee if the errant employee will 'at least try and better himself [sic]'.[73] Indeed, the 'choice' of the recalcitrant employee to become involved with the EAP services becomes the 'litmus test' for some employers as to whether they want this person to remain employed.[74] Some have suggested figures for these supervisory referrals as being as high as 30 per cent or 40 per cent of the total of EAP referrals.[75]

Troubled workers may be identified by supervisors.[76] Policy guidelines for use when a manager or supervisor recognises a continuing or repeated deterioration in work-performance are proffered by many.[77] What is rendered here is a generalised overview of the coercive referral process, the essence of which appears to be followed by many. The supervisor or manager is reminded to be alert to (and watch for) excessive absenteeism; persistent lateness; deteriorating relations with colleagues; actions adversely affecting the work and safety of others; an uncharacteristically high error-rate; a high accident-rate; or the abuse of flexi-time.[78] Those 'observed' to be deficient in one of these areas are summoned for an initial 'formal' interview where, it is stressed, personal and private problems should not be discussed. The supervisory focus should be upon deciding on measures the errant colleague should take to improve their performance. A 'factual', written record of this interview is taken, which contains only 'relevant' information. This is provided for supervisors and may be signed by (or simply shown to) the officer involved.[79] Most importantly, the supervisor must advise the officer that if work-performance has not improved to a 'satisfactory' level by the time of the next interview, the officer will be referred immediately to a more senior level.[80] The reader is reminded of the difficulties in determining what 'satisfactory' and 'factual' might mean.

The 'interview' process proceeds through several (generally, three or four) phases if performance does not 'improve' to a 'satisfactory' level. Work-performance may be continually 'monitored' and 'controls maintained' during this period by the more senior staff member.[81] The unsatisfactory performer is 'encouraged' throughout this process to seek counselling or other treatment via the EAP. Staff *should* be reminded that this action would not prejudice future job-security or promotional opportunities.[82] However, concurrently, they may also be reminded that failure to seek such 'help' can lead to termination.[83] Where 'appropriate', the advice of the errant worker's professional counsellor(s) may be sought through the EAP provider, as was the case for Hank.[84]

The managerialist agenda: EAPs as instrumental 'tools'

As noted above, EAPs are, significantly, regarded as 'cost control tools'; 'productivity tools'; 'risk management tools' – all components of productivity and efficiency.[85] Trice and Beyer assert that EAPs are a relatively recent addition to the procession of performance-oriented managerial innovations.[86] Many of these management 'innovations' are expressions of currently popular ideologies rather than applications of scientifically-proven facts.[87] In this case, the performance-based ideologies that have swept the United States workplace this century, combined with the demonstrably strong relationship between managerial support for EAPs and managerial ideology, serve to support a symbiotic structure that perpetuates and strengthens the use of EAPs.[88] If the programmes do not work, then the fault is assumed to lie – not with the service and its unchallenged dogma – but with the 'problem worker'. For example, 20 per cent of the workforce at one organisation was laid off and yet the EAP programme was retained as it was assumed that the EAP 'magic wand' was still working.[89]

There have been concerns raised about the instrumental application of emotionality in organisations. Hochschild has commented on the increasing use of emotional labour in organisational life; that emotional labour is a key feature of the work that many people do; that a smile, a display of friendliness have, in many instances, become integral parts of the job.[90] Gordon has suggested that it is a cheap option for an employer, in the 'smiling business' (such as in the hospitality industry), to pay for counselling to assist in the resolution of personal problems.[91] In the context of EAP usage, one sees that 'coercive' referrals to EAPs may be made for those perceived to 'need' it: the emotional; the depressed; the unhappy; the morose; the unfriendly. 'Negative' emotions may still be regarded as disruptive and dysfunctional in many quarters, as the blossoming EAP industry confirms. In Hank's case, for example, he was judged to be insufficiently pleasant and enthusiastic.

EAPs as panopticist practices: Concerns with social control revisited

Hank's surveillance by his new manager, in collaboration with Human Resources and the EAP consultant, was panopticist – he did not know his behaviours ('positive' or 'negative') were being watched, how they were being judged, or when. The outcomes of the intervention, which in Hank's case could have resulted in his dismissal, were subjective, value-laden, and managerialist. The panopticist, modern organisation where overt, corporal punishment has been replaced by surveillance, is demonstrated: a surveillance where the watched are unaware they are being watched.[92] In modern workplaces, modern managers embrace the task of 'judging' normal behaviour using their positional power. EAP coercive referrals provide a vivid illustration. Hank submitted to the intervention planned for him. What choice (other than resigning) did he have? The surveillance, in this case, reinforces the need for actors to acquiesce, to 'appear' flexible and untroubled by organisational stressors, and to 'mask' any 'undesirable' emotionalism they may be experiencing. It was deemed unacceptable that Hank be uncomfortable and unhappy with his perceived demotion. The organisation stepped forward to help him 'resolve' his discomfort.

Others have noted concerns with EAPs as a form of social control.[93] The use of EAPs embodies certain shared values and beliefs – a common ideology – that suggests that a combination of compassion and concern for performance is appropriate when dealing with emotionally-troubled employees.[94] EAPs are also referred to as a 'gatekeeping function' for counselling and the EAP discourse confirms and supports notions of social and human engineering.[95] For example, Mapstone refers to the need to 'maintain' people – the engineering approach to human capital – with the justification supported axiomatically: far less money is being spent on people maintenance than equipment.[96] As EAPs increase their institutional presence and their marketing drive, one might be inclined to revisit the 'old story' of social engineering, as devised by the Human Relationists. The EAP industry is characterised more by internal struggles for customers, power and dominance than by a sense of community or concerned action.[97] Given the rise of managerialism, its associated human costs and its influence on the increasing implementation and utilisation of EAPs, one must return to issues of social control.[98]

EAPs as instruments of control

Hopkins has suggested that the employee assistance movement is an attempt to integrate the conflicting ideological themes of social control and humanitarianism.[99] The abundant insights on institutional coercion, paternalism and the shaping of 'deviants' into more appropriate and workable moulds, especially for those who are regarded as in some way non-functional, are vast and should be revisited as EAPs become, increasingly, a means of leverage over the 'recalcitrant' or 'deviant' – another instrumental outcome of modernity and industrialisation, and a means for colonising and commodifying the behaviour, thoughts and feelings of organisational actors.[100]

Foucault's analyses of power in organisations shed light on the portent of EAPs as instruments of control. One notes the move from the tortures, gibbets, gallows and pillories of the eighteenth century to the multiple network of diverse elements – walls, space, institution, rules, discourse – that make up the new 'carceral city'.[101] Expertise is called in through the psychiatrist (or, in EAPs, also a psychologist, counsellor or other health-care worker) in order to imply judgements of normality, attributions of causality, assessments of possible changes and anticipations as to the offender's future.[102] Hank's story provides an exemplary case. Indeed, the supervision of disease (among which alcohol and drug abuse are now included)[103] is inseparable from a whole series of other organisational controls: 'the military control over deserters, fiscal control over commodities, administrative control over remedies, rations, disappearances, cures, deaths, simulations'.[104]

If one returns to Bentham's vision of the Panopticon, one notes that actors in the Panopticon are under inescapable surveillance.[105] The object is seen but does not see. Those coerced into the use of EAPs become the objects of information, rather than subjects of communication. The unverifiable nature of the surveillance means that the 'client' of the EAP will not know when or whether they are being observed. The EAP (metaphorically depicted as a Panopticon) becomes a mechanism of power reduced to its ideal form.[106] Using the metaphor directly, in the Panopticon's 'peripheric ring' (where the worker is figuratively scrutinised), the object is totally seen without ever seeing. In the central tower (where supervisor, management and counsellors figuratively reside), the observers see everything without ever being seen.[107] The Panopticon was also a laboratory used to carry out experiments, to alter behaviour, to train and correct individuals – a privileged place for experimentation with complete certainty in the transformations required.[108] Hank's 'improvement' in behaviour might provide a case-in-point.

Given the managerialist, the social engineering and power-oriented agendas portrayed above, it is interesting to observe that the use of EAPs tends, almost exclusively, to be directed towards the lower levels of the organisation. The problematic return to paternalism and social control, through the threat of referral, is usually made only to the lowest levels of the organisation, highlighting the supervisory control of the decision and action process with 'coercive' use of EAPs.[109] As a supervisor, one is charged with *identifying* the 'problem employee'.[110] One has to wonder who is 'observing' the pathological and problematic supervisor. Unsurprisingly, resistance to the programmes multiplies at the lower levels of the organisation.

The need for confidentiality in the use of EAPs is widely acknowledged and documented, perhaps significantly contributing to the propaganda.[111] Confidentiality is said to be the 'key' to the success of EAPs,[112] the 'cornerstone' of its effectiveness.[113] However, when one critically scrutinises associated practice, some 'confidentiality challenges' become manifest. Whilst there is no question that, most of the time, the records of counselling sessions and 'formal' performance evaluation sessions are kept strictly confidential, occasionally, this may not always eventuate.[114] Dickman suggests that there are numerous ways to break confidentiality without even trying: by scheduling clients from the same industry (or company) too close together; by maintaining rigid nine-to-five counselling hours necessitating that clients ask for time off work; by randomly assigning clients to group-support sessions without checking with them first; by allowing (indiscreet) clerical verification of employment from mental health centres or drug treatment centres; by allowing EAP co-ordinators to visit employment sites (and recognise current or former clients); by contacting clients, inappropriately, at work to change appointments; and by telling referring supervisors more than necessary.[115]

When the performance evaluation of a recalcitrant worker continues through the various stages of interview and observation,[116] it is acknowledged that, occasionally, managers seek the advice of counsellors when reviewing the case of the especially intractable staff member.[117] This advice should always be preceded by a request for permission from the troubled worker under review, although the pending threat of termination might provide sufficient incentive to induce compliance to this request. In any event, the only information that should be passed on is whether the staff member kept the appointment, whether they (in the opinion of the counsellor) need 'treatment', and whether they have accepted or rejected the recommended treatment.[118] Hank's case confirms that this is not always what transpires.

EAPs, Plato's Cave and the 'new breed' of supervisor

Plato's work *The Republic* and the famous allegory of the cave, where Socrates addresses the relations among appearance, reality and knowledge, is a stark reminder of the problem of flawed perceptions and knowledge.[119]

The allegory pictures an underground cave with its mouth open toward the light of a blazing fire. Within the cave are people chained so that they cannot move. They can see only the cave wall directly in front of them. This is illuminated by the light of the fire, which throws shadows of people and objects onto the wall. The cave dwellers equate the shadows with reality, naming them, talking about them, and even linking sounds from outside the cave with the movements on the wall. Truth and reality for the prisoners rest in this shadowy world, because they have no knowledge of any other.[120]

The difficulty arises when one accepts the shadowy world of the cave as being representative of 'truth' and 'reality'. Organisational actors are constrained by the thinking, the values and the ideological foundations of their adjacent social and institutional arenas. Supervisory judgements about a subordinate's 'normal' behaviour will be influenced accordingly. Observations made are shaped by the socially-created nature of social life with reality being produced by human beings (and all of their faulty knowledge and beliefs) as an interpretive mesh of individuals and groups.[121] The EAP surveillance imperative demands that one 'judge' another and their apparent normality, just as transpired for Hank. However, one cannot reasonably consider a person's behaviour or experiences without considering the ways in which those environments have influenced that person's experiences of them.[122] The 'truth' of the observations will be based on the 'facts', as seen by the viewer, which may be very different from those observed by another. Questions arise as to the objective capability of any individual, their selective perception (seeing what they want to) and how personal biases might influence the supervisor in this role.[123] The inevitably flawed nature of supervisory 'observation' becomes apparent.

The supervisor's role is crucial in providing support to employees with personal problems so that work productivity is not adversely affected.[124] However, the supervisor may also be a major source of stress.[125] Further, the assumption of rationality (that is, using reason and logic) and objectivity on the part of the observing supervisor or manager is problematic. Decisions and judgements are made that are driven by the values, attitudes, beliefs, norms, mores and perceptions (complete with their inherent attributional biases or political agendas).

These decisions are, according to current organisation myth, rationally made and implemented.[126] However, familiar stories from the 'real-world'[127] continue to confirm that the official image of formal organisations, including the idea of how they are structured, how the actors within them behave, how they should behave and how the work processes unfold, is completely alien to the stories one continues to hear about organisational life.[128] One might conclude that supervisors are rarely as 'rational' or 'objective' as one might be led to believe.

There is a 'new breed of supervisors'[129] required during the 'age of reorganisation' in 'lean and mean' organisations.[130] Supervisors play a critical role in humanising organisations through responding to workers' work and family dilemmas, and facilitating workers' use of family support policies and programmes.[131] However, it is also acknowledged that, in many instances, supervisors do not confront troubled workers even when their problems appear quite severe and the question remains unresolved as to whether supervisors should intervene at all.[132]

Conclusion

The authors are not advocating a removal of EAPs. In many circumstances, EAPs provide a useful service to support staff at all levels during traumatic life events. EAPs can certainly offer support for staff in crisis situations, whether organisationally related or not. However, the possibilities for EAPs being used in other, less helpful ways, are manifest. Sanctioned coercion through the use of 'coercive referrals' allows a means of managerial legitimisation of attempts to 'reshape' individuals. Further, the inappropriate connections between the content of counselling or assistance sessions, or even the notification of their existence, would seem to vivify the possibilities for panopticist practices by management over staff at lower levels in the organisation. We are reminded of possible outcomes where the watched do not know they are being watched.

Further research is warranted. Given the brief analysis of Hank's case, qualitative research is suggested involving *recipients* of EAP referrals, both from the self-referred and, more importantly, from those involved with 'coercive referrals'. In this way, the 'voice' of those who may have been subjected to coercive practices under a paternalistic and humanitarian guise might be free to speak of their possible feelings of violation, betrayal and anger. Difficulties may be encountered by a researcher interested in sharing these stories: opposition from the EAP providers as well as mistrust from those who have been part of the 'coercive referral' process.

Notes

1. M. Foucault, *Discipline and Punish: The Birth of the Prison*, Vintage Books, New York 1977, p217.
2. W.G. Emener, 'Human Resource Development in Employee Assistance Programming: An Overview', in W.S. Hutchison, and W.G. Emener (eds), *Employee Assistance Programmes: A Basic Text*, Charles C Thomas Publisher Ltd, Springfield 1997a, pp231-237.
3. M. Rose, *Industrial Behaviour*, Penguin, United Kingdom 1982, p103.
4. P. Thompson, *The Nature of Work: An Introduction to Debates on the Labour Process* (2nd edition), Macmillan Education, Hampshire and London 1989, p18.
5. P. Thompson and D. McHugh, *Work Organisations: A Critical Introduction*, Macmillan Education, Hampshire and London 1990, p24.
6. *Ibid*.
7. M.M. Harmon and R.T. Mayer, *Organisation Theory for Public Administration*, Chatelaine Press, Burke, VA.1986, p198.
8. W. Hollway, *Work Psychology and Organisational Behaviour*, Sage, London 1991, p82.
9. C. Williams, *Beyond Industrial Sociology: The Work of Men and Women*, Allen and Unwin, Sydney, Australia 1992, p25.
10. T.J. Watson, *Sociology, Work and Industry* (2nd edition), Routledge, London and New York 1987, p54.
11. W.S. Hutchison and W.G. Emener, 'Part I: History and Philosophy', in W.S. Hutchison and W.G. Emener (eds), *Employee Assistance Programmes: A Basic Text*, Charles C Thomas Publisher Ltd, Springfield 1997, p3.
12. H.M. Trice and J.M. Beyer, 'Employee Assistance Programmes: Blending Performance-Oriented and Humanitarian Ideologies to Assist Emotionally Disturbed Employees', *Research in Community and Mental Health*, 4, 1984, p267; R. Reynes, 'Programmes That Aid Troubled Workers', *Nation's Business*, June, 1998, p73.
13. *Ibid*.
14. T.D Hartwell, P. Steele, M.T. French, F.J. Potter, N.F Rodman, and G.A Zarkin, 'Aiding Troubled Employees: The Prevalence, Cost, and Characteristics of Employee Assistance Programmes in the United States', *The American Journal of Public Health*, 86, 6, 1996, p804.
15. For an in-depth analysis of these terms see respectively: H. M. Robinette, *Burnout in Blue: Managing the Police Marginal Performer*, Praeger, New York 1987, p24; S. Isenberg, 'The EAP Model in Lincoln, Nebraska', *Proceedings of the Third Occupational Drug and Alcohol Programmes Conference*, Melbourne (October 10-12, 1983) 1984, p30; T.D. Hartwell et al, *op. cit.*,

p804; R. Ballard, 'An In-House EAS: An Outline of the Employee Assistance Service, Department of Education, Queensland', *Proceedings of the Third Occupational Drug and Alcohol Programmes Conference*, Melbourne (October 10-12, 1983) 1984, p67; S.B. Bacharach, P.A. Bamberger and W.J. Sonnenstuhl, 'MAPs: Labor-Based Peer Assistance in the Workplace', *Industrial Relations*, 35, 2, April, 1996, p261; F. Dickman and B. R. Challenger, 'Employee Assistance Programmes: A Historical Sketch', in W.S. Hutchison and W.G. Emener (eds), *Employee Assistance Programmes: A Basic Text*, Charles C Thomas Publisher Ltd, Springfield 1997, p54. Our emphasis.

16. T. D. Hartwell et al, *op. cit.*, p804; K. M. Hopkins, 'Supervisor Intervention with Troubled Workers: A Social Identity Perspective', *Human Relations*, 50, 10, 1997, p1216.

17. R. Reynes, *op. cit.*, p73.

18. H.M Robinette, *op. cit.* p5; our emphasis.

19. H.M. Trice and M. Schonbrunn, 'A History of Job-Based Alcoholism Programmes 1900-1955', in W.S. Hutchison and W.G. Emener (eds), *Employee Assistance Programmes: A Basic Text*, Charles C Thomas Publisher Ltd, Springfield 1997, p8.

20. S. Isenberg, *op. cit.*, p30; K.M. Hopkins, *op. cit.*, p1221; H. M. Trice and M. Schonbrunn, *op. cit.*, p10.

21. F. Dickman and B.R. Challenger, *op. cit.*, p51.

22. H.M. Trice and M. Schonbrunn, *op. cit.*, p34.

23. S. Isenberg, *op. cit.*, p30.

24. R. Ballard, *op. cit.*, p67; W.M. Burgess, 'Development of a Public Service Alcohol and Drug Programme: From A Union Perspective', *Proceedings of the Third Occupational Drug and Alcohol Programmes Conference*, Melbourne, (October 10-12, 1983) 1984, p58; K. M. Hopkins, *op. cit.*, p1217.

25. W.M. Burgess, *ibid.*; T.J. Callaghan and B. Tydings, 'Instant Gratification', *Occupational Health and Safety Library*, 67, 10, October 1998, p132; R. Ballard, *op. cit.*, p67.

26. S. Isenberg, *op. cit.*, p31.

27. H.M. Trice and M. Beyer, *op. cit.*, p250.

28. K.M. Hopkins, *op. cit.*, p1222.

29. B.R. Challenger, 'The Need for Employee Assistance Programmes', in W.S. Hutchison, and W.G. Emener (eds), *Employee Assistance Programmes: A Basic Text*, Charles C Thomas Publisher Ltd, Springfield 1997, pp45-46.

30. P. Kline, *Psychology and Freudian Theory: An Introduction*, Methuen and Company Ltd, London 1984, p20; M. Oldham and B.H. Kleiner, 'Understanding the Nature and Use of Defence Mechanisms in Organisational Life', *Journal of Managerial Psychology*, 5, 5, 1990, ppi-iv.

31. H.M Trice and M. Beyer, *op. cit.*, p253.

32. T.D. Hartwell et al, *op. cit.*, p807.

33. R. Reynes, *op. cit.*

34. *Ibid.*, p73; M.E. Oss and J. Clary, 'The Evolving World of Employee

Assistance', *Behavioral Health Management*, 18, 4, July-August, 1998, p20; F. Marks, 'Drug and Alcohol Dependence in the Workforce – Legal Implications', *Proceedings of the Third Occupational Drug and Alcohol Programmes Conference*, Melbourne (October 10-12, 1983) 1984, p10; A.S. Brooks, *Occupational Health and Safety Law in Australia* (4th edition), CCH Australia Limited, Sydney 1993.

35. T.J. Callaghan and B. Tydings, *op. cit.*, p132.

36. F. Marks, *op. cit.*, p10; A.S. Brooks, *op. cit.*; WorkCover New South Wales, *Drugs, Alcohol and the Workplace*, WorkCover Authority of NSW, Sydney 1995, p4.

37. M.R. Gottlieb and L. Conkling, *Managing the Workplace Survivors: Organisational Downsizing and the Commitment Gap*, Quorum Books, Westport 1995, p5.

38. M.W. Oss and J. Clary, *op. cit.*, p20.

39. *Ibid.*

40. *Ibid.*, p23.

41. J. Henderson, 'How to Support Grief and Loss in the Workplace (Workforce Tools)', *Workforce*, 76, 9, September, 1997, pp3-5.

42. T. D. Hartwell et al, *op. cit.*, p807.

43. W.G. Emener, 'Service Delivery: Implications for the Utilisation of Programme Evaluation Information', in W.S. Hutchison and W.G. Emener (eds), *Employee Assistance Programmes: A Basic Text*, Charles C Thomas Publisher Ltd, Springfield 1997b, p206.

44. R. Ballard, *op. cit.*, p67.

45. M.W. Oss and J. Clary, *op. cit.*, p20.

46. J. Gordon, 'Avoiding the Litigation Trap: Tips on Minimizing Risk in Employee Work/Life Programmes', *Forbes*, 162, 10, 2 November, 1998a, p68; J. Gordon, 'The New Paternalism', *Forbes*, 162, 10, 2 November, 1998b, p69.

47. H. M. Trice and M. Beyer, *op. cit.*, p247.

48. J. Gordon, *op. cit.*, 1998b, p68.

49. W.G. Emener, *op. cit.*, 1997a, p236.

50. W. Umiker, 'Staff Career Development Programmes: The Role of Supervisors', *The Health Care Supervisor*, 17, 1, September, 1998, p12.

51. K.M. Hopkins, *op. cit.*, p1223.

52. *Ibid.*, p1224.

53. M.R. Gottlieb and L. Conkling, *op. cit.*, p91.

54. H.M. Trice and M. Beyer, *op. cit.*, p245; K.M. Hopkins, *op. cit.*, p1225.

55. See, for example, K.M. Hopkins, *op. cit.*, p1225; J. Gordon, *op. cit.*, 1998b.

56. K.M. Hopkins, *op. cit.*, p1224.

57. L. McClure and W.B. Werther, 'Violence at Work: Consultants and Managers Walking the Line', *Journal of Workplace Learning: Employee Counselling Today*, 9, 6, 1997, pp211-214.

58. *Ibid.*, p213.

59. *Ibid.*

60. *Ibid.*

61. *Ibid.*

62. L.T. Eby and K. Buch, 'The Impact of Adopting an Ethical Approach to Employee Dismissal During Corporate Restructuring', *Journal of Business Ethics*, 17, 12, 1998, pp1253-1264.

63. M.W. Oss and J. Clary, *op. cit.*, p21.

64. See K.M. Hopkins, *op. cit.*, p1224; our emphasis.

65. R. Ballard, *op. cit.*, p67.

66. H.M. Trice and M. Beyer, *op. cit.*, p254.

67. *Ibid.*, p267.

68. V. Donald and C. Sturgess, 'Occupational Assistance Service, Melbourne and Launceston', *Proceedings of the Third Occupational Drug and Alcohol Programmes Conference*, Melbourne (October 10-12, 1983) 1984, p85; R. Reynes, *op. cit.*, p74.

69. H.M. Trice and M. Beyer, *op. cit.*, p254.

70. *Ibid.*, p251.

71. *Ibid.*

72. R. Reynes, *op. cit.*, p74.

73. *Ibid.*

74. *Ibid.*

75. S. Isenberg, *op. cit.*, p33; Donald and Sturgess, *op. cit.*, p85; M. Davis, 'Department of Aviation's Staff Assistance Scheme: A National Approach', *Proceedings of the Third Occupational Drug and Alcohol Programmes Conference*, Melbourne (October 10-12, 1983) 1984, p54.

76. WorkCover, *op. cit.*, p7.

77. W.M. Burgess, *op. cit.*; H. M. Robinette, *op. cit.*,p24; WorkCover, *op. cit.*, pp8-9.

78. W.M. Burgess, *op. cit.*, p60.

79. *Ibid.*, p61.

80. *Ibid.*

81. *Ibid.*, p62.

82. *Ibid*; R. Reynes, *op. cit.*, p74.

83. R. Reynes, *ibid.*

84. W.M. Burgess, *op. cit.*, p64.

85. M.W. Oss and J. Clary, *op. cit.*, p21.

86. H.M. Trice and M. Beyer, *op. cit.*, p246.

87. *Ibid.* p245.

88. *Ibid.*, p246.

89. S. Isenberg, *op. cit.*, p34.

90. R. Hochschild, *The Managed Heart: Commercialization of Human Feeling*, University of California Press, Berkeley 1983; *ibid.*; Y. Gabriel, 'Psychoanalytic Contributions to the Study of the Emotional Life of Organisations', *Administration & Society*, 30, 3, July, 1998, p292.

91. J. Gordon, *op. cit.*, 1998b.

92. J. Bentham, *The Works of Jeremy Bentham: Volume IV* (edited by J. Bowring),

Edinburgh 1843, p40; M. Foucault, *op. cit.*, p203.

93. See, H.M. Trice and M. Beyer, *op. cit.*; K.M. Hopkins, *op. cit.*
94. H.M. Trice and M. Beyer, *op. cit.*, p262.
95. M.W. Oss and J. Clary, *op. cit.*, p21.
96. D. Mapstone, 'Interlock – Occupational Counselling and Training Services', *Proceedings of the Third Occupational Drug and Alcohol Programmes Conference*, Melbourne (October 10-12, 1983) 1984, p49.
97. H.M. Trice and M. Beyer, *op. cit.*, p263.
98. S. Rees, 'The Fraud and the Fiction', in S. Rees and G. Rodley (eds), *The Human Costs of Managerialism: Advocating the Recovery of Humanity*, Pluto Press Australia, Sydney 1995a, p16; S. Rees, 'Greed and Bullying', in S. Rees and G. Rodley (eds), *The Human Costs of Managerialism: Advocating the Recovery of Humanity*, Pluto Press Australia, Sydney 1995b, pp197-210; K. Solondz, 'The Cost of Efficiency', S. Rees and G. Rodley (eds), *The Human Costs of Managerialism: Advocating the Recovery of Humanity*, Pluto Press Australia, Sydney 1995, pp211-220; M.H. Vickers, '"Sick organisations", "Rabid Managerialism": Work-Life Narratives From People with "Invisible" Chronic Illness', *Public Voices*, 4, 1, 1999, pp59-82; M.H. Vickers and A. Kouzmin, '"Resilience" in Organisational Actors and Re-Articulating "Voice ": Towards a Humanistic Critique of New Public Management', *Public Management*, 3, 1, forthcoming.
99. K.M. Hopkins, *op. cit.*, p1225.
100. See for example, M. Foucault, *Madness and Civilization*, Tavistock Publications, London 1961; M. Foucault, *op. cit.*,1977; T.S. Szasz, *The Manufacture of Madness*, Granada Publishing, Suffolk 1970; T. Szasz, *The Theology of Medicine: The Political-Philosophical Foundations of Medical Ethics*, Syracuse University Press, Syracuse 1977/1988; T. Szasz, *Sex: Facts, Frauds and Follies*, Basil Blackwell, Oxford 1980; I. Illich, *Medical Nemesis: The Expropriation of Health*, Marion Boyars, London 1975; B.S. Turner, *Medical Power and Social Knowledge*, Sage Publications, London 1987; J.H. Skolnick, 'Sheldon L Messinger: The Man, His Work, and The Carceral Society', in T.G. Blomberg and S. Cohen (eds), *Punishment and Social Control: Essays in Honor of Sheldon L Messinger*, Aldine de Gruyter, New York 1995, p19.
101. M. Foucault, *op. cit.*, 1977, p307; J.H. Skolnick, *ibid.*, p19.
102. M. Foucault, *ibid.*, p20.
103. M. Davis, *op. cit.*, p52.
104. M. Foucault, *op. cit.*, 1977, p144.
105. Cited in M. Foucault, *op. cit.*, 1977, p200.
106. *Ibid.*, p205.
107. *Ibid.*, p202.
108. *Ibid.*, p203, p204.
109. K.M. Hopkins, *op. cit.*, p1225, p1226.
110. See for example, S. Isenberg, *op. cit.*, p30; I.O. Spicer, 'Opening Address for Australian Foundation on Alcoholism and Drug Dependence',

Proceedings of the Third Occupational Drug and Alcohol Programmes Conference, Melbourne (October 10-12, 1983) 1984, pp1-2; H. M. Robinette, *op. cit.*, p4; WorkCover, *op. cit.*

111. R. Ballard, *op. cit.*, p67; W.M. Burgess, *op. cit.*; V. Donald and C. Sturgess, *op. cit.*, p84; WorkCover, *op. cit.*; F. Dickman, 'Ingredients of an Effective EAP', in W.S. Hutchison and W.G. Emener (eds), *Employee Assistance Programmes: A Basic Text*, Charles C Thomas Publisher Ltd, Springfield 1997, p78; W.G. Emener and W.S. Hutchison, 'Professional, Ethical and Programme Developments in Employee Assistance Programmes', in W.S. Hutchison and W.G. Emener (eds), *Employee Assistance Programmes: A Basic Text*, Charles C Thomas Publisher Ltd, Springfield 1997, p335.; *ibid.*, pp330-351.

112. G. Grammeno, 'Employee Assistance Programmes', *Occupational Health and Safety Library*, Book 6, Series 1, June, 1998, p8; R. Reynes, *op. cit.*, p74.

113. F. Dickman, *op. cit.*, p78.

114. W.M. Burgess, *op. cit.*

115. F. Dickman, *op. cit.*, pp78-81.

116. W.M. Burgess, *op. cit.*; WorkCover, *op. cit.*

117. See, for example, W. M. Burgess, *op. cit.*, p64.

118. F. Dickman, *op. cit.*, p81.

119. Cited in G. Morgan, *Images of organisation* (2nd edition), Sage Publications, Thousand Oaks 1997, p215.

120. *Ibid.*, pp215-216.

121. A. Schutz, *The Phenomenology of the Social World*, Northwestern University Press, New York 1932/1967; P.L. Berger and T. Luckmann, *The Social Construction of Reality: A Treatise in the Sociology of Knowledge*, Allen Lane, London 1966.

122. J.W. Osborne, 'Some Basic Existential-Phenomenological Research Methodology for Counsellors', *Canadian Journal of Counselling*, 24, 2, 1990, p80.

123. V. Donald and C. Sturgess, *op. cit.*, p88.

124. K.M. Hopkins, *op. cit.*, p1217.

125. R. Bolton, *People Skills: How to Assert Yourself, Listen to Others and Resolve Conflicts*, Simon Schuster, Sydney 1987.

126. O.C. McSwite, 'Stories From the 'Real World': Administering Anti-Administratively', in D.J. Farmer (ed), *Papers on the Art of Anti-Administration*, Chatelaine Press, Burke 1998, pp7-36.

127. *Ibid.*, p25.

128. O.C. McSwite, *op. cit.*, p26.

129. K.M. Hopkins, *op. cit.*, p1216.

130. M.R. Gottlieb and L. Conkling, *op. cit.*, p3; *Ibid.*, p5; A. Davis, 'Managerialised Health Care', in S. Rees and G. Rodley (eds), *The Human Costs of Managerialism*, Pluto Press Australia, Sydney 1995, p125; A. Kouzmin, N. Korac-Kakabadse and A.M. G. Jarman, 'Economic

Rationalism, Risk and Institutional Vulnerability', *Risk, Decision and Policy*, 1, 2, December, 1996, pp229-256.

131. K.M. Hopkins, *op. cit.*, p1218.
132. *Ibid.*, p1222, p1218.

Dimensions of a critical psychology of learning and teaching

Arnd Hofmeister

This paper examines different dimensions of the relationship between learning and teaching from a critical psychological point of view, in order to gain new ideas for a critical psychology of teaching. The focus is on the conceptualisation of the learner, the teacher and the learning-object, as well as the learning-teaching relation and the institutional background. These reflections remain in an area of conflict, because, on the one hand, concepts of teaching have to be improved and on the other, especially in school, the repressive function of teaching-processes is apparent in the selection and ideological formation of people.[1] This fundamental contradiction is responsible for many problems within educational practices.

Mainstream constellations

The following stereotyped descriptions of mainstream research in learning and educational psychology should not be understood as a simplifying critique but as an attempt to work out the basic structure and organisation of this kind of research. Most theorists and practitioners in this field provide very elaborated, and sometimes even critical, theoretical accounts of learning and teaching, but when it comes to practice, they often just refer to simple behaviourist and cognitivist assumptions. Within mainstream psychology and pedagogy, learning and teaching processes are conceptualised as if they are simple processes of instruction in which a teacher prepares and imparts knowledge or competences to a learner who assimilates them with different levels of success. The learner's relation to the world is not reflected systematically: s/he appears as an isolated individual, whose interest and motivation exist without any connection to the world. Mainstream psychological and educational accounts[2] do not understand motivation as the specific emotional relation of the individual to the world in his /her process of societalization.[3] Instead, what appear as theories of the learner are actually theories of teaching. On closer inspection the teacher is reduced to a teaching function within the apparatus of learning and teaching. Theoretically, the relation of learning and teaching is conceptualised as if everything which is taught is or has to be learned immediately. The teacher is expected to develop a curriculum which makes the subject-matter attractive to the students. The learning-object is a world of ready-made facts and solved problems, which have to be brought into a sequence following the epistemological principle that knowledge is structured from the simple to the complex. The learning-teaching relation is understood as a set of variables which explains this relationship (e.g. the enthusiasm of the teacher, the empathy with students, coping styles of students and so on). This does not adequately reflect the social, economic and ideological context in which learning and teaching takes place. The school is treated as though it were a laboratory; the learner is reduced to a experimental subject; the teacher is the experimenter; and the experimental process is legitimised by reference to method. The educational system in modern capitalist societies is legitimised by its function of selection and allocation of people. The procedures of teaching and assessing are taken to guarantee the basic liberal-democratic principles of equality and individuality.[4] In Germany, educational theorists tend to use ethical or anthropological arguments to justify the school as a site of learning and teaching which can be understood as separate from its social, economic and ideological function.

The positivist functionalist character of this mainstream approach to learning and teaching processes, with its lack of understanding of history and society, (re-)produces an isolated individual and utterly fails to grasp human subjectivity as a manifestation of the concrete relationship between the individual and society.[5] These theories are deeply rooted in the Fordist formation of society, which has been paradigmatic from the 1930s to the 1970s for Western Europe and North America.

This formation is characterised by a relatively stable social structure and correspondingly stable forms of individuality. This structural background is a necessary (but not sufficient) condition for understanding why learners and teachers behave in particular ways, as if learning were simply mechanistic. The move into neoliberalism and postfordism, at once both more heterogeneous and contradictory, poses a considerable problem for the traditional theories/technologies of learning and teaching. In my view, the task of a critical psychology is to criticise theoretically and delegitimise politically these conceptualisations of learning and teaching. Therefore, Critical Psychology has to develop a theoretical framework, in which learning and teaching problems may be analysed in a non-individualistic way, but which understands them as part of the complex individual-society relation.

Critical theorising of learning processes

In his book, *Learning. A Subject-Scientific Foundation*, Klaus Holzkamp offers an explanation of learning processes from the subject's point of view, that is, from the perspective and the motives of the learner.[6] While behaviourist S-R theories and cognitivist approaches conceptualise learning processes in an objectivist manner as something imposed on subjects and controlled by the conditions, Holzkamp's theory attempts to take account of the agency/subjectivity of the learner, analysing learning-processes in their contradictory social context, and to develop concepts with which learning problems can be understood in both their individual specificity and their societal relatedness. His theory provides analytical tools to understand why, for example, in particular circumstances, people are motivated to enlarge their knowledge and competences, while in others, they just resist demands and opportunities for learning. The traditional distinction between intrinsic and extrinsic motivation does not allow a further understanding of such contradictions because it simply reifies intrinsic motivation as a drive, without asking for the individual's objective premises and subjective grounds for acting, and thus it individualises learning problems. By contrast, the subject-scientific theory of learning attempts to investigate the premises on which the tendency to act either way is grounded in the subject's relation to the world.[7]

For Holzkamp learning is the basic human capacity for enlarging one's own 'action-potence'[8] in society in order to improve one's quality of life. Incidental learning occurs as an unintended, coincidental effect in everyday practice, while intentional learning, which he focuses on, is the specific attempt to broaden one's own knowledge and competences in order to overcome problems of acting. A 'problem of acting' thus generates a 'problem of' or 'for learning'. In addition, the discrepancy between the pre-learned actual knowledge and competences and the learning-object cannot consist only of their objective difference, but has to be experienced by the subject as such. As to the emotional-motivational dimension behind learning activities, Holzkamp differentiates between different grounds for learning. On the one hand, learning activities may be motivated by anticipation, in that the subject is empowered through learning to expand his/her influence over essential life circumstances (action-potence) and thus to improve his/her quality of life. In this case Holzkamp speaks of 'expansive grounds for learning'. On the other hand, where such prerequisites for intentional learning activities are missing, the blunt rejecting of any learning activity would bring with it a threat even to the subject's currently-available action potence. If, in these circumstances, the subject were forced to learn, that learning would, of necessity, be defensive.[9] If, for example, one had to take an English test and there were deep aversions to any learning, the learning activity would be geared towards passing the test and not towards improving one's language capacities; this learning process is defensively grounded. The subject only learns to prevent or abate threats to his/her self-efficacy. In the case of defensive grounds for learning, the intention of the subject is not primarily directed at solving a genuine learning-problem, but at managing a precarious situation. Theoretical approaches which try to induce motivation usually fail, in so far as they try to persuade the individual to internalise external compulsion.[10]

On the cognitive dimension, Holzkamp tries to develop a categorical framework with which the specific structure of intentional learning processes can be analysed. Although the subsequent description of this structure is ideal-typical, it allows an understanding of problems within learning-teaching relations. In such ideal situations, where a subject identifies and accepts current difficulties of acting as deficits that can only be overcome by a learning-process, s/he separates a 'learning-loop' at the end of which s/he anticipates mastering this problem with his/her new knowledge or competences. This learning loop can be studied either operatively or thematically, i.e., in terms of the functional organisation of the learning process or its contents. The operative aspect is subordinate because the intention of learning is primarily focused on the content, with which the subject expects to be able to overcome the acting problem. For Holzkamp, the operative organisation is itself determined by the structure of the subject-matter. (The current pedagogical demand that pupils have to learn principles of learning is a false abstraction so long as it does not take account of the specificity of subject-matters to which such principles refer. There is an important difference between learning logical thinking in a mathematical or philosophical context or as part of learning Latin or computing.) Having identified a specific learning problem and its subject-matter, the subject actualises specific dimensions of this learning-object. These need not at first correspond to its objective structure, but the more the subject studies this learning-object, the deeper s/he comprehends its structure; s/he finally gets an adequate idea of this learning-object.

As a realist project, Holzkamp's learning-theory presupposes that via expansively-grounded learning processes the subject gets, step by step, an adequate or sufficient idea of this subject-matter. In the long run, this process leads from the 'immediacy' to the 'societal mediatedness' of this learning-object in the form of qualitative steps.[11] But the concrete process of learning is not single-track in the sense of being from the simple to the complex, but rather discontinuous.[12] The steps of a learning process have to be conceptualised from the subject's point of view and not, as in most instruction-theories, from the teacher's point of view or from the presumably-clear structure of the learning object itself. There is a difference between this approach and those following Piaget or Vygotsky. Piaget's theory, as a genetic epistemology, describes different levels of cognitive development but not the subject's learning process, in which s/he changes from one level to another. Ulman pointed out that teaching practices which refer to Piaget misunderstand his test-exercises as training exercises.[13] They often, for example, just test whether the child has developed an abstract idea of numbers, instead of supporting this development. Vygotskian approaches which refer to his concept of the zone of proximal development have a normative idea of individual learning processes. Even though they focus on the learning subject, these zones are conceptualised from a teacher's perspective.

However, there is a tension between the realist understanding of society, in which the subject actively socialises him/herself through learning, and the strict focus on the subject's perspective while theorising processes of societalisation. This contradicts any normative idea that learning processes have a specific aim. This tension finds concrete expression in the reconstruction of individual learning and societalisation processes and cannot be dissolved theoretically within the framework of German critical psychology.[14]

While learning, the subject notices the insufficient character of his/her old learning-principle, its old comprehension of the learning-object; s/he has to change from a definitive process of learning, in which the learning-object and the structure of the learning process is clear, to an affinitive one. Affinitive means in this context that the subject has to develop a new perspective upon the learning-object, to discover its wider connections in the field of knowledge. The process is associative without any transparent structure. This is different for metacognitive approaches, which conceptualise metacognitive processes as a cognitive function of reflection over one's own processes of thinking.[15] For Holzkamp, the cognitive reflections of learning activities are not separate as an extra level of learning, because they are themselves part of the intentional learning process. Learning without any self-reflection and self-comment is more of an incidental than of an intentional kind.

The most important difference between a subject-scientific theory of learning and mainstream psychological concepts is the systematic connection between the subject-matter of learning processes and the motivation for learning. It is therefore necessary for a critical psychology of teaching to have an idea of the epistemological structure of knowledge.

'Learning-objects' in postmodern conditions

The development of German Critical Psychology is deeply rooted in the critique of positivist epistemology. This critique did not simply focus on its misconception of human subjectivity but also on the positivist concept of truth and the objectivity of scientific knowledge. The problem of mainstream psychology of learning and teaching, which is based on this positivist scientific ideal, is not only its suspension of subjectivity, but also its world view, in which contradictions, conflicts and ambivalences are hardly thinkable. The world is conceptualised in these theories as an ensemble of known facts and solved problems. A closer look at curricula demonstrates how deeply this epistemological idea structures learning and teaching realities. The critique of positivist epistemology has changed in the postmodern turn. The idea of replacing the positivist by a dialectical epistemology and thereby developing an adequate concept of subjectivity and objectivity is regarded as historically and theoretically delegitimised. The world in postmodern theory is conceptualised as a contradictory and ambivalent net of discursive and non-discursive practices, which cannot be brought into order without structuring the discourse in a theoretically violent way.[16] Such thinking, with its focus on the over-determination of the subjective perspective on the world and self, corresponds with the subject-scientific theory of learning. Postmodern epistemology is a viable basis for the differentiated analyses of the structure of learning processes from the subject's perspective, because it allows a very detailed reconstruction of the learner's train of thought with its possibilities and problems, as well as a re-definition of the teacher's tasks.

According to the postmodern critique of modern epistemology, the claim to bring knowledge into a strict order is problematic. However, starting from the Lyotardian thesis of the strict plurality of discourses, epistemology has to look for transitions between different discourses, not for their absolute mediation.[17] The problem of this heterogeneity of discourses becomes evident in case of a conflict between two discourses where there is no rule to dissolve this conflict, because each solution would ignore the specific quality of at least one discourse. The task of the philosopher or the teacher as an intellectual is to look for an idiom to articulate this conflict in an adequate way.[18]

Against this epistemological background and its critique of positivism, there are new possibilities for conceptualising learning and teaching processes. In expansive processes of learning, the subject notices that his/her understanding of the learning-object is insufficient. In a postmodern discourse-theoretical perspective there are many possibilities to connect this learning-object with other discourses. This connection is first of all as legitimate as others. It is an open question on which connections the learner draws. It is not determined by the positivist objective structure of the learning-object, but more the result of the irreducible spontaneity of subjectivity. Imagine any subject-matter and then the questions which arise from it. There will not be only one way, but multiple perspectives to continue working on this issue. The idea of a clear structure of knowledge and its disciplinary constitution is to be understood as the result of the spread of disciplines with all their measures of ordering, as described by Foucault.[19] Individual learning processes do not create the world in a new way, but take place within a discursive and non-discursive field. It is the task of the teacher to question these constructed connections within the field of knowledge, whether they bring this knowledge into a simplifying order, which ignores its contradictions and ambivalences, or how to draw other connections, which would allow new insights.

Critical reflections on teaching processes

If we compare these reflections about learning processes with theories of teaching, we find a similar neglect of the teacher as a subject of teaching processes. Instructional theories and dominant conceptions of teaching practice suppose that the teacher prepares the learning-objects, which are fixed by curricula. S/he has therefore to phrase the general and specific aims of the learning or teaching process and then to structure the learning-object into forty-five minute sequences. Finally s/he tries to find adequate media so the learners will be able to take on the given knowledge or competences. At the end there is an examination, which documents the success of this process. In brief, teaching means structuring a specific amount of knowledge in a motivating way to make the pupils or students learn it. This stereotyped description may sound a little bit casual, but unfortunately analyses of actual German teaching methods and of the lesson-concepts and analyses of post-graduate student-teachers have shown that, for example, each lesson is separated into five-minute sequences, for which the teacher has to specify the goals and the methods, questions and the right answers.[20] The general rhythm of such lessons is the classical three-step: exposition, development and recapitulation. There is no space for spontaneity or creativity, which goes beyond this structure.

The teacher does not appear as an interested subject, but is functionalised as a transformer of knowledge (the fantasies of programmed learning are still very much alive). At the same time, the teacher is the manager of the supposed learning-process. Holzkamp describes this conception as a 'learning teaching short-circuit', which assumes that the learner learns everything which is taught. Differences in learning success are naturalised as talent or, conversely, individualised as the incompetence of the teacher. These conceptions of lessons are geared towards a normal, average pupil, who is a scientific fiction. Such concepts demonstrate their middle-class, white, male and Eurocentric basis. Their ideological functions and the way they reproduce symbolic power are evident.[21]

Research programmes which investigate specific traits of teachers and their behaviour, misconstrue the relation of emotionality and the taught subject-matter. Abrami, Leventhal & Perry analysed the influence of teachers' enthusiasm on teaching-processes.[22] They conceptualised emotionality as an independent variable and looked for its relation to learning success. But in their operationalisation there was no difference between an abstract enthusiasm/emotionality and a specific kind of interest in a subject-matter. Multivariant approaches to learner-teacher relations distinguish between different teaching-styles (the classical definition refers to Bussis & Chittenden[23]). But even the distinction between open and directive teaching-styles remains abstract so long as the structure of the subject-matter and its relation to the whole context of the learning-teaching relation is not reflected systematically: to put it in philosophical terms, there are times to introduce or summarise in a directive way and there are times to leave space for individual questions and developments.

A critical psychology of learning and teaching has to develop instruments for analysing learning-teaching processes and for thinking about alternatives. The basic requirement for an expansive learning-teaching process is an interest in the learning-object. The attempts to produce motivation usually fail, resulting in a form of defensive and resistant learning (see above) on the part of the learner, who tries to avoid situations where his/her self-efficacy is threatened, and which form part of the power-relations of teaching situations. Parallel to the concept of defensive learning, there is a form of defensive teaching. While preparing and running the lessons, the teacher has to take into account many judicial regulations and curricular norms. Furthermore, s/he is asked to follow specific instructional concepts and standard ideas of a good lesson. In consequence, we find this form of defensive teaching, which is the result of the contradiction between the pedagogical impulse, (the so-called idealism of teachers,) the institutional regulations and the force to assess' which in the end leads to the carrying out of a standard programme. Interviews with teachers have shown that they often try to avoid subject-matter with which they have theoretical difficulties or in which they are not interested.[24] Against this background, curricula not only cause problems in learning-processes but also in teaching processes. Furthermore, these interviews show the eminent importance of 'learning-objects' while theorising learning and teaching processes. The motivation for learning *and* teaching is grounded in the subject-matter as a part of the world, in which both parts of this process try to keep or enlarge their action-potence.

The general force to assess leads to some paradoxical demands on teachers: they should recognise the individuality of their pupils, but they have to assess according to standard-norms; they need to have personal contact with each pupil, but they have to have distance for assessing; they need pedagogical interactions to be open and communicative, but the institutional regulations and curricular norms make this more difficult. These paradoxical demands cannot be solved, but have to be reflected while analysing teaching problems.[25] These reflections should be part of the teaching situation itself; making these structures lucid opens up the possibility for a critical dialogue instead of reciprocal instrumentalisations.

In instruction theories the interest of the learner is seldom taken into account and usually reduced to a general evaluation of their interests.[26] Such evaluations are in themselves problematic, because it remains unclear what happens to those interests which are not taken into account. This leads to a resistance to lessons on the part of the learner, because s/he assumes that the teacher follows his/her own ideas. Hence the evaluation of interest seems for him/her to be nothing more than a democratic front to hide power-relations. Even where a teacher presents the chosen subject-matter, this may cause problems, because s/he transforms it according to his/her perspective and assesses the results. Such transformations can be experienced as a kind of expropriation of the learners' interest.

Even the ideal concepts of a good lesson cause many problems. A lesson is regarded as successful when the pupil follows the teacher's train of thought in a disciplined way to perform a learning 'discovery'. For the learner this leads either to the impression of manipulation or, in the worst case, to a guessing game where the learner has to guess what the teacher wants to hear. Furthermore, following the thesis of the heterogeneity of knowledge, there is no learning-object which has a clear structure. At each moment of the teaching process, the learner can follow his/her own train of thought, which may give the impression, that he or she is not concentrating, although it reflects the learning-object in another way. Discourse analyses of classroom interactions brought out that often short interactions between pupils show that they try to understand the learning object with phrases like 'what does he mean?' though teachers often feel they are simply chatting.

The problem of the concept of 'discovery learning'[27] is its insufficient reflection on the institutional background of learning-teaching relations. First of all, this is less a learning theory and more a teaching theory, teaching understood as an intentional organisation of learning conditions. The moments of freedom in this learning process depend on the educational criteria of the teacher. For Bruner, the aim of discovery learning is *to make the pupil* into an autonomous and spontaneous thinker.[28] This is a contradiction in terms. The identification of the initiation of a discovery-process and the result of such learning effects (e.g. autonomy) ignores the subjectivity of the learner, who has to transform such a teaching requirement into his/her own learning-problem for developing ideas of what freedom of learning may mean.

The critique of teaching processes should not be misunderstood as implying that teachers are unnecessary or that teaching is impossible. Their extensive knowledge of their subject and its heterogeneity as well as their competence in structuring questions allows them to give advice while the learner acquires a special learning-object. The knowledge of the teacher should not be misunderstood as expert knowledge, but as something practical, which consists not only of facts, but more of questions, problems and contradictions within a specific field. It gets its practicality because it is a condition *sine qua non* of individual action-potence. Action-potence means 'the exercise of control by the individual over his or her own requirements of life through participation in the control of the societal process'.[29] The teacher's task is to reflect the learner's train of thought critically and to take care that insights in specific relations of knowledge should not be generalised in a problematic way. In this sense, his or her epistemological task is to show the conflicts which arise in processes of arranging knowledge or discourses.[30]

Constructivist approaches talk, in relation to teaching processes about the possibility of the perturbation of learning systems.[31] Following the idea that each individual constructs his or her own world, the possibility of instruction is unthinkable. Perturbation means, in this context, to disturb the individual's order, to ask new questions and suggest other perspectives. The problem of such individualistic conceptualisations is the neglect of individual agency in its relation to social necessities and the practical character of human action. The constructivist approach does not reflect the institutional regulation of learning and teaching processes. The concepts remain *idealist*: to focus in teaching processes more on the perspective of construction than the perspective of instruction; to talk about a didactic of facilitating, which leaves more space for the learner to reflect, etc. The simple comment that such a teaching method collides with the official task of teaching knowledge signals a problem which is crucial for a critical re-thinking of teaching processes.[32] The result of constructivist teaching methods in actual school practice probably consists of rankings of the most innovative construction or in the demand on pupils to use silence for reflecting the problem. (Holzkamp often quoted ironically a pupil's question: 'Miss, do we have to do what we want now?'). Furthermore, constructivist approaches do not reflect the interest of the learner, the emotional-motivational dimension of learning processes. Emotionality in constructivist theory is often nothing more than an important but unspecific amount of energy with contingent relations to cognition[33] and has to be reflected in teaching processes strategically from the teacher's point of view. This theoretical separation allows one to develop parts of a teaching method with a complementary co-existence of instruction and construction, which allows construction for those who are intrinsically motivated and instruction for those who are less *interested/intelligent*.[34]

In co-operative learning-teaching relations the subjective perspective of the teacher becomes more important, as does his/her specific approach towards his/her subject-matter and formulation of questions. In consequence, after a period of individual or collective research and discussion his/her task consists of collecting the acquired knowledge and showing new perspectives. He/she can even refer to dimensions of knowledge which are not immediately comprehensible provided he/she realises that everything which is taught need not be learned.

While reconstructing individual learning processes, it becomes evident that they are not the result of continuous learning efforts (see above). In this context, teaching may as well be described as sending a 'message in a bottle'.[35] When a teacher explains something which is not immediately understood or which criticises a concrete perspective of the learner, this leads to an irritation of the individual's world-view. These explanations are rejected. Yet they continue existing in the memory, isolated by misunderstanding or defence. However, they may appear sometimes in another context, where they produce immense learning effects. These ideas do not release the teacher from self-critique, but they show that the self-obligation to be always understandable is not right from a learning-theoretical point of view. Teaching means asking questions rather than giving answers.

In this context the traditional lecture gains importance because it orients the learners about a specific learning-object. However, it would be a misunderstanding if, afterwards, the audience were expected to remember everything which was said. It has a meditative function, where the audience gets new ideas and follows their own train of thought. It would be a rehabilitation of this classroom interaction if there were enough space for one's own reflections without control and examination. Teaching here means to open and enlarge the horizons of thinking.

'Critical pedagogy' often pointed out the problematic character of the social inequalities in relation to race, class and gender, which are reproduced within learning and teaching processes.[36] This critique led to curricular revisions and to the critique of forms of lectures. These inequalities never change in school, but there are possibilities of making this symbolic power visible, which is important for its critique.[37] The concept of project-work in a group-oriented classroom takes the critique of critical psychology seriously. This classroom-style does not structure the learning-object in a homogeneous way, but allows different approaches, in which the learners develop their own formation of questions. The results are heterogeneous and correspond to the supposed structure of knowledge. Even if the teacher summarises the results in the end, the learners are able to notice what the teacher thinks is important and what s/he leaves out. The subjective perspective of the teacher plays an important role which may serve the reproduction of social inequalities, but at the same time the differentiated knowledge of the learners allows criticism of power relations, without remaining abstract.

A critical psychology of learning and teaching has to criticise concepts which suppose that learning and teaching processes can be controlled, and should show their regulating and suppressing character. It has to develop a new culture of learning and teaching. To me this task seems possible at this moment, in which societies are said to be transformed into so called 'information societies'. These new spaces should be shaped actively instead of leaving them to those who work on the reproduction of subjected subjects.

Notes

1. Hofmeister, 'De-Construction of Subjectivity and Psychological Subject-Science', in W. Maiers, B. Baier, B. Duarte Esgalhado et al. (eds), *Challenges to Theoretical Psychology*, Captus University Publications, North York, Ontario 1999, pp450-456.
2. Bandura, *Social Learning Theory*, Prentice Hall, Englewood Cliffs, N.J 1977; L. Petersen, *Stop and Think Learning: A Teacher's Guide for Motivating Children to Learn, Including Those with Needs*, Acer, Cumberwell 1995.
3. Ch. W. Tolman, *Psychology, Society and Subjectivity, An introduction to German Critical Psychology*, Routledge, London 1994, pp37-38.
4. N. Luhmann, 'Codierung und Programmierung, Bildung und Selektion im Erziehungssystem', in H.E. Tenorth (ed), *Allgemeine Bildung, Analysen zu ihrer Wirklichkeit, Versuche über ihre Zukunft*, Beltz, Weinheim 1986, pp154-182.
5. Ch. W. Tolman, *op. cit.*, p52.
6. K. Holzkamp, *Lernen , Subjektwissenschaftliche Grundlegung*, Campus Verlag, Frankfurt / New York 1993.
7. *Ibid.*
8. K. Holzkamp, 'Societal and Individual Life Process', in Ch. W. Tolman and W. Maiers (eds), *Critical Psychology, Contributions to an Historical Science of the Subject* Cambridge, University Press, New York / Cambridge 1991, pp50-64.
9. K. Holzkamp, 'Lernen und Lernwiderstand – Skizzen zu einer Subjektwissenschaftlichen Lerntheorie', *Forum Kritische Psychologie*, 20, 1987, pp5-36.
10. Ch.W. Tolman, *op. cit.*, p121.
11. Ch.W. Tolman, 'Critical Psychology: An Overview', in Ch. W. Tolman and W. Maiers (eds), *Critical Psychology, Contributions to an Historical Science of the Subject* Cambridge, University Press, New York / Cambridge 199, pp1-22.
12. G. Ulmann and I. Dierks, 'Zum Thema "Evaluation Universitärer Lehre" ', *Forum Kritische Psychologie, 38*, 1997, pp80-92.
13. G. Ulmann, 'Zahlbegriff versus Rechnen – oder "Handlungsmagik" und

Probleme der "Identitaut"', *Forum Kritische Psychologie 38, 1997*, pp35-53.

14. A. Hofmeister, '*Zur Kritik des Bildungsbegriffs aus Subjektwissenschaftlicher Perspektive, Diskursanalytische Untersuchungen*', Argument, Berlin 1998.

15. J.H. Flavell, 'Metacognition and Cognitive Monitoring: A New Area of Cognitive-Developmental Inquiry', *American Psychologist, 34*, 1979, pp906-911.

16. M. Foucault, *L'ordre du discours*, Éditions Gallimard, Paris 1972.

17. J. F. Lyotard, *Le Différend*, Les Édition de Minuit, Paris 1983.

18. H. Giroux, 'Teachers as Transformative Intellectuals', *Social Education, 49*, 1985, pp376-379.

19. M. Foucault, *Surveiller et punir. La Naissance de la Prison*, Éditions Gallimard, Paris 1975.

20. W. Klafki, 'Die bildungstheoretische Didaktik im Rahmen kritisch-konstruktiver Erziehungswissenschaft' in H. Gudjons and R. Winkel, *Didaktische Theorien*, Bergmann and Helbig, Hamburg 1997, pp11-26; W. Schulz, 'Die Lehrtheoretische Didaktik', in H. Gudjons and R. Winkel, *Didaktische Theorien, op. cit.*, pp29-45; , Ch. R. Möller, 'Die Curriculare Didaktik', in H. Gudjons and R. Winkel, *Didaktische Theorien, op. cit.*, pp63-77; R. Winkel, 'Die kritisch-kommunikative Didaktik', in H. Gudjons and R. Winkel, *Didaktische Theorien, op. cit.*, pp79-93.

21. P. Bourdieu and J. C. Passeron, *Grundlagen einer Theorie der symbolischen Gewalt*, Suhrkamp, Frankfurt/Main 1973.

22. P.C. Abrami, L. Leventhal, & R. P. Perry, 'Educational Seduction', *Review of Educational Research, 52*, 1982, pp446-464.

23. A.M. Bussis and E.A. Chittenden, 'The Teachers' Manifold Roles', in Ch. E. Silberman (ed), *The Open Classroom Reader*, Random House, New York 1973.

24. Gehrmann, *Widerstände von Lehrern beim Unterrichten schwieriger Themen*, Unpublished Master's Thesis, University of Heidelberg 1998.

25. W. Helsper, 'Antinomien des Lehrerhandelns in modernisierten pädagogischen Kulturen. Paradoxe Verwendungsweisen von Autonomie und Selbstverantwortlichkeit', in A. Combe, W. Helsper (eds), *Pädagogische Professionalität, Untersuchungen zum Typus pädagogischen Handelns*, Suhrkamp, Frankfurt/Main 1996, pp521-569.

26. Klafki, Schulz; see H. Gudjons and R. Winkel, *op. cit.*

27. J.S. Bruner, 'Der Akt der Entdeckung', in H.Neber (ed), *Entdeckendes Lernen*, Beltz, Weinheim 1973, pp15-27.

28. *Ibid.*, p17.

29. K. Holzkamp, *Grundlegung der Psychologie*, Campus, Frankfurt/Main 1983, p241; translated by Ch. W. Tolman, *Psychology, Society and Subjectivity, An Introduction to German Critical Psychology*, Routledge, London 1994, p241.

30. J. F. Lyotard, 'Der Philosophische Gang', in P.Engelmann (ed), *Grabmahl des Intellektuellen, Jean Francois Lyotard*, Böhlau, Graz / Wien, 1985, pp40.52; F. Haug, 'Erfahrungen in die Krise führen – oder Wozu brauchen die Lernenden die Lehrer', in *Die Wertfrage in der Erziehung*, Argument, Berlin 1981.

31. H.U. Maturana and F.J. Varela, *Der Baum der Erkenntnis, Die biologischen Wurzeln der Menschlichen Erkenntnis*, Goldmann, München 1990.

32. H. Siebert, *Pädagogischer Konstruktivismus Eine Bilanz der Konstruktivismusdiskussion für die Bildungspraxis*, Luchterhand, Neuwied 1999, p42.

33. L. Ciompi, *Die Emotionalen Grundlagen des Denkens, Entwurf einer Fraktalen Affektlogik*, Vandenhoek & Ruprecht, Göttingen 1997, pp95-99.

34. G. Reinmann-Rothmeier and H. Mandl, 'Lehren im Erwachsenenalter', in F.Weinert, H. Mandl et al. (eds), *Enzyklopädie der Psychologie Bd.4, Psychologie der Erwachsenenbildung*, Hogrefe, Göttingen 1997, pp355-390.

35. The term 'message in a bottle' refers to the self-characterisation of the writings of the Frankfurt School especially M. Horkheimer and T.W. Adorno. It meant the attitude of writing without having an audience, for an unspecific future, where they might be understandable. I would like to transfer this metaphor to the structure of more concrete learning-teaching relations.

36. H. Giroux, *op. cit.*

37. P. Bourdieu and J. C. Passeron, *op. cit.*

A critical psychology for split subjects, drives, and theorising acquaintance rape prevention

Kareen Ror Malone

This paper reviews the conceptual basis of current prevention programmes in acquaintance rape. It looks at the strategies of such programmes, contemporary research on the effectiveness of such programmes and current ideas on why rape happens. The paper suggests that, theoretically at least, researchers are beginning to ask some interesting questions about how cognition and the body 'work' together to create sexual aggression. Rape research in psychology has, in recent decades, been informed by feminism and consequently, a certain social sensibility pervades such research. But such broadened social and theoretical awareness may go nowhere if one does take up seriously the theoretical question of subjectivity and the body (gender being a moment of this question). Clearly feminism has, in some respects, addressed this issue. Psychoanalytic feminism, whether from Lacan or object-relations, has focussed more exclusively on the very point where the body, desire, and subjectivity meet. Using a Lacanian approach, the paper ends with an explication of some notions, the drive and the Other, to add another dimension to theorising acquaintance rape and its prevention. It is hoped that such ideas may generate alternatives to attitude research that may otherwise simply end up in very traditional conceptualisations.

The first research paper on sexual violence within dating relationships appeared in 1957.[1] With the continuing press of second-wave feminism through the seventies, and incremental but consistent scholarly attention to sexual assault between known parties, both the legal system and public consciousness began to shift toward the recognition of the problem of acquaintance rape. This recognition challenges a number of earlier assumptions about the nature of rape. As data on acquaintance rape accrued, it became clear that a rapist is more likely to be a man whom the woman knows, who will, in committing the rape, only threaten force or simply ignore the woman's protests. When the research of Mary Koss and others indicated the extent of sexual assault and attempted rape on college campuses in the United States, the emerging consciousness of the actual nature of rape came to include the knowledge of its nearly epidemic proportions.[2]

On college campuses, approximately 25 per cent of women have experienced what could be legally considered rape or attempted rape. This result is widely replicated throughout the Western world.[3] On the other side, between 5 to 14 per cent of college men report behaviours that meet the legal definition of rape and college athletes and fraternity members are even more likely to rape than the average college male. Research indicates that rapists will repeat such behaviors.[4] Thus college students represent a very high-risk group.[5] However, they live in a community where the possibilities of organised intervention and research are far more viable than with some other sectors of the population.[6] As a result, the 1980s saw the wide proliferation of acquaintance rape prevention programmes.

Emergency phones appeared outside libraries; more lighting was installed; bushes were pruned near walk-ways. These tactics obviously have their limits when it comes to a rape that occurs at someone's home, at a party and in the context of a broader if superficial interpersonal relationship. So unless colleges were willing to institute more aggressive forms of *loco parentis*, the points of intervention had to lie with changing the behaviours of college men and women.

In response to these parameters, efforts at prevention began to focus on 'psycho-education'. Such programmes were loosely based on facilitators' beliefs about attitude change and frequently on their feminist orientation in the understanding of the causes of rape. Programmes that target women teach assertiveness and emphasise communication skills in a sexual situation. A good number focus on men: their ideas of masculinity, the legal definition of rape and increased sensitivity to the communications and needs of their partners.[7] Others try a mixed-sex approach. Typically, programmes include a video depicting a date rape, discussion of that video and the presentation of local statistics on rape. Given recent research on rapists and empathy, a victim-empathy training session, role-playing, or some other experiential exercise is included. Many of the ideas that inform acquaintance rape prevention, especially as directed to men, who after all are the perpetrators,[8] blend a feminist analysis with a broad-brush incorporation of strategies directed toward attitude change. In most programmes, there is also a very strong overall focus on clear communication in sexual situations.

A review in the early nineties found over one thousand different approaches in acquaintance rape prevention programmes.[9] Although clearly many participants find such programmes enlightening,[10] there is very little empirical substantiation of any changes in rates of sexual victimisation and assault by participants.[11] Furthermore, attitude-change is left unmeasured or is only measured directly after the intervention. Follow-up surveys render contradictory findings but usually indicate that self-identified perpetrators and victims remain unchanged by such programmes and that attitudes and awareness for some other groups 'rebound' after a couple of months.[12]

As one might expect from North American mainstream social psychology, there have been a number of calls for better research. Less predictably, there have also been a number of calls to further theorise about the motivations of rapists and thus what sorts of interventions would best target this group.[13] This uncharacteristic sensitivity to psychology's theoretical limits, at least in this case, reflects the interdisciplinary roots of current thinking on rape, which draws upon feminist legal theory and feminist theory in general, itself a disciplinary hybrid.[14]

Feminist-inspired research suggests that seeing acquaintance rapists as deviant individuals with serious psychopathology is erroneous.[15]

Thus, despite the traditional default of psychology toward a-contextual analyses, most psychologists who research rape clearly perceive the cultural and political horizon that must inform research and interventions in this area.[16] As a consequence of this broader social awareness, a certain political sensibility typically frames the deployment of the relevant psychological constructs. Many researchers in the field understand cultural constructions as inherent to the 'psychological' data that they are investigating, suggesting that critiques of reigning notions of masculinity and patriarchy are intrinsic to their efforts at intervention and research. This means that such research has, in a sense, recognised the social link.

> Rape is not an isolated behaviour, but a behaviour linked in men's lives to larger systems of attitudes, values, and modalities of conduct that constitute masculinity. In this model, rape prevention work begins with men and with men's questioning of prevailing assumptions about masculinity and their re-thinking what it means to be a man. I am extremely sceptical of any rape prevention programme work that proposes solutions to the problem of rape but leaves masculinity, as we know it, largely intact.[17]

With its origins in feminism, prevention research borders on a repudiation of the typically psychologising movement that understands the psychological within the terms provided by the individual. Thus, research on acquaintance rape apparently belies the usual political critique of mainstream research, its 'relentless focus on the individual ....'[18]

In some respects, then, those working within the field of acquaintance rape are deviating from the usual conceptual confines of traditional North American psychological theory. But are they really? Is a recognition of the effects of socially-constructed gender roles and the conditions of oppression that serve as their support sufficient? Constructs such as adversarial sexual beliefs and adherence to traditional gender roles, while correlated with sexually aggressive behaviours and certain sorts of responses to sexual scenarios, are still just attitudes; they are social constructions that may be targeted in prevention but they are not a theory of sexual aggression. Without such a theory, prevention programmes eclectically take up certain strategies and forego others (more on this below). Often after a nod to cultural effects, the question simply becomes, how do we persuade recalcitrant men that their adherence to rape myths and adversarial beliefs about heterosexuality should be given up? Should we rely on central-route processing or other models of persuasion?[19] The tenets of attitudinal research become the *psychological* theory upon which such programmes implicitly rely.

Once one ventures into motivations, things become even murkier. On the one hand, it is presumed that rape-prone beliefs are maintained because they are functional for such men (how?). On the other hand, it is asserted that such attitudes are imbued with intense (dysfunctional?) emotion.[20] Moreover, one is still at a loss when inquiring how these gender attitudes become so essential to some male subjects.

In fact, delegating such notions to the realm of attitudes leaves major questions unaddressed in that the concept of attitudes often functions as a psychological garnish to an unexamined notion of the self. Simply seeing these attitudes as socially derived does little that is radical in the complex theorisation that is required to understand the intersection of the social and the body. The imputed autonomy of the individual *qua* stuffed envelope of attitudes and attributes subtly re-enters as the backdrop of these disciplinary discourses.

This return of the individual, while recognising the political dimension, means that one's political interests can be compromised by a form of psychological equalisation, i.e., women sexually harass men: is it the same?[21] Furthermore, a default to a notion of an individual with attitudes represses the subject's own fragile constitution, its basis in self-deception, its desires and inconsistencies. Even empirical research discovers this divided and inconsistent subject.[22] The conclusion that traditional research cannot conceive is that its notion of individuality, from which subjects regularly deviate, is simply a societal suture. In exact parallel to this careless appropriation of a social category lies a theoretical lacuna; this (empty) idea of the individual has always functioned in psychology as a cover for a lack of theorisation of the relationship between culture and human experience, desire, and the body.

In acquaintance rape research, the complicated nature of such 'attitudes' and their relationship to such intangibles as the 'body', becomes painfully obvious in that these attitudes putatively condition these men's sexual fantasies, their sexual arousal, and for some men dictate their sexual behaviour. Given this, it seems requisite to theorise not only attitudes but also the structure of subjectivity and the meaning of gender – how gender sticks to a body. The domain of acquaintance rape has been initially politicised, and so it should be, but a task remains: to better understand the linkage between the social and the subjective as a proper object of research, conceptualisation and intervention.

Subjectivity and gender

From the arguments above, it is at least justifiable to begin any critical evaluation of acquaintance rape programmes with a theoretical discussion of the questions of subjectivity and gender. In this paper, subjectivity and gender are approached through the disciplinary lenses of feminism and psychoanalysis. The significance of feminism is at one level obvious. Feminism has been relatively successful in re-framing legal and social responses to rape and will be at the forefront of further reforms. At another level, one can also turn to feminism for its astute attention to that cusp between the social and the body, that intimate inscription that we call gender.

> Since feminism begins in the home, so to speak, as a collective reflection on practice, on experience, on the personal as the political, and on the politics of subjectivity, a feminist theory only exists as such insofar as it refers and constantly comes back to these issues.[23]

Nonetheless, some reasonably argue that theories of social change would be more important tools for feminism or critical psychology than feminist and/or psychoanalytic conceptions of subjectivity; the detour into subjectivity takes too long.[24] But to forego the question of the subject may presume too much clarity with regard to a psychologist's contribution to human emancipation.

The question of subjectivity in relationship to political aims becomes quite pressing when one deals with issues such as acquaintance rape prevention. Prevention programmes imply forms of psycho – education. These forms may be ameliorative and salutary. They may incorporate a political horizon, but they are not without unexamined horizons regarding the meaning of sexuality, subjectivity, and gender. Let us take the issue of sexual aggression as particularly germane. A great deal of qualitative and quasi-clinical research suggests that rape is motivated by some desire for revenge[25] and by a competitive and identificatory relationship to other men that is somehow mediated by forced sex with a woman (the elimination of the question of her desire). What do such observations tell one about the structure of masculine sexuality and sexual arousal? There aren't many answers in current research.

Researchers within traditional psychology have noted that one of the motivations for rape is 'physiological arousal' in response to (mis)perceived hostility.[26] Men with a willingness to engage in rape or those who have raped perceive women as hostile even when other men perceive the same behaviours as seductive or friendly. Then these 'rape prone' men find the hostility arousing. To refer to this dynamic as 'arousal in response to hostile cues' begs the question. It fails to theorise the relationship of patriarchal entitlement and the perceptions of deprivation, hostility, and humiliation that these men report.[27] At one level, we are dealing with the narcissism of patriarchal privilege. At another level, these men fantasise a (socially inexplicable) deprivation, get angry, and get aroused. Such attributions give women unreal and unrealisable power that certain men feel they must vanquish. The production of this scenario is arousing.

What is it in the structure of Western patriarchal masculinity that creates a group of men for whom some formation of hatred is sexually arousing? What is it that they hate? It may be essential to push certain feminist queries and ask if hate may entail certain structures that are in turn related to the 'core' questions of gender identity and sexual aggression.[28] Some authors implicitly suggest that *all* men (one in three fantasise about rape) want to rape but most possess an ability to invoke 'inhibitory' self-talk.[29] Let's look at this explanation. This explanation presumes some self-interested biologically-wired man attracted to a woman who serves as the natural sexual outlet.[30] But in the process of positing 'testosterone-challenged' men, one not only elides the dimension of the political; one ignores the constitutive relationship between sociality, the body, and subjectivity. Also, one covers over the paradoxical conditions of arousal and inserts a biological hypothesis of instinctual gratification.

At the level of prevention, one relies on discovering effective cognitive strategies that would increase inhibitory self-talk in the targeted group of men. With this sort of intervention, the turn to psychology has led to a number of very traditional precepts about gender and subjectivity. The former becomes biological and the latter is characterised as some recognisable distribution between cognition and physiology. Even traditional psychologists are left to wonder how this contraption works.[31]

I would argue that a loss of any feminist perspective or even any political perspective also follows from this same failure to theorise the mediation between culture and body, this mediation being the problem of subjectivity. Within psychology at least the theoretical vacuum will be inevitably filled in certain predictable ways, ways that suppress broader cultural questions.

The turn to psychoanalysis

Positing the irreducibility of subjectivity is very typical of psychoanalytic feminists. Nancy Chodorow notes that 'the concerns in the emotional realm, gender related or not, are tied up with (at least our society's) notions of human fulfilment – selfhood, agency, meaningful relationship, depth and richness of experience, a comfortable centring in our bodies and in our sexuality'.[32] Chodorow is using very broad categories, which leaves her open to certain ideological defaults – for instance: selfhood – and to presuming the complex gratifications that reside there – comfort, centring. Chodorow's introductory *qua* phenomenological rendition of the dimension of the subjective appears as a foil to her early, more Marxist, political stance. But Chodorow's problem here lies not with the assertion of some irreducible realm of effects outside of traditional notions of the political but rather with how she theorises or doesn't theorise those subjective effects.

Following a recurring division within feminism, Aida Hurtado counters that this pre-occupation with the subjective evident, for example, in Chodorow's quotation is more compelling to WMCFs (white middle-class feminists) who must psychologically adjust to close proximity with patriarchal privilege.[33] Such women are exploited differently and less than those who are explicitly dis-enfranchised by the social order. Although important, Hurtado's observations are, in my opinion, limited. For certainly all persons must attach to community and at some point fail to do so. Said differently, bodies must enter into an intersubjective logic in order to function and misfire in recognisably human ways. Such simultaneous failure and interpellation are the very processes that have attracted some within politics and feminism to psychoanalysis and/or to Lacanian views despite the problems that many see as resident there. A structural understanding of subjectivity does not equal a concern with contentment and the most significant subjective effects may not be directly experienced at all. If psychoanalysis becomes a phenomenology, it will forego its particular contribution to social analysis. Nor does a concern with such effects preclude other political considerations or an attention to particular cultural histories and experiences.

The question of the subjective is essential for those of us who are oriented to the sorts of social transformation that overlap with concerns that often have been designated as private matters, such as sexuality and the body. Furthermore, in social changes that entail psycho-educative efforts, the change agent directly aims to subjective transformation, usually by re-framing signifiers of identity (gender in acquaintance rape prevention) or by re-framing communicative patterns in a situation involving sexuality – a sort of mind/body/Other problem. In exploring the constitution of sexuality and identity, theorists have entertained questions of fantasy, corporeality, and psychoanalysis.[34] I would like to add to this list the question of the drive and the spilt subject.

These are Lacanian notions and one can only introduce such ideas briefly. If identity at its point of instantiation is balanced against an absorption into the Other – its symbolic genesis – one way to understand identity is as a defence against the Other's asymmetrical right to enjoy me and refuse me (not laugh at my jokes, not listen to me, see me any way he wishes). The Other as the locus of the signifier (source of language, culture, law) is complicated by its incarnation in some particular other and by the impossibilities of the Symbolic Order itself (full of holes, an impostor, and so forth). Although the perception of the Other/other as a subject might mean that I can withstand this other *jouissance* (enjoyment) through the medium of desire, it also means that I can experience this *jouissance* as insatiable in relation to me as its object (no matter what I give you, you are not satisfied). Rape it seems bears a relationship to this *jouissance* of the Other: the other steals the man's *jouissance* or the perpetrator will give the woman *jouissance* that she is demanding but won't allow. By contrast, *nobody* imagines that the victim enjoys being robbed but rapists and even normative men often fall prey to a fantasy scenario where the woman enjoys it.

More broadly, research into sexuality and power, sexuality and aggression is littered with what are called non-conscious effects. A percentage of women will sleep again with a man who has raped them in the context of a date.[35] Although a very viable argument can be made that this statistic merely reflects the cultural conflation of desired heterosexual intercourse and forced sex, one might, giving women a more complex subjectivity, understand other sorts of dynamics at work, in terms of which women find themselves in a complicated network of determinative forces out of which they must emerge as desiring beings.[36] On the other side, men who are likely to sexually harass women are more likely to respond to power cues as arousing, without seeming to register such fantasies consciously.[37]

Since masculinity is the primary risk-factor for being a rapist, we must ask how the masculine processes of identification and these questions of the Other and *jouissance* have become entangled at this particular historical juncture. Although a number of feminist approaches have critically examined the interdependence of cultural formations and masculinity, these approaches presume attributes such as self-interest and an uncomplicated acquiescence to social prescriptions. Thus one can argue that Catherine MacKinnon's characterisation of sexuality as an effect of patriarchal power erases the problematic of feminine desire and really of anyone's desire as an ethical question.[38] Subjective positions are collapsed into the Symbolic Order. To supplement the difficult project of understanding the mediation between culture and human desire may require some singular reflections on subjective structures.

For Lacan, of course, the subjective dimension is linked to language. No signifier, no subject.[39] Given that Lacanian approaches presume that language links sociality, consciousness, subjectivity, desire, and unconscious inscriptions that instantiate the body, it is assumed by some feminists that the Lacanian approach is the most promising for a social theory.[40] But the failure of the signifier, the difficulty of the unsayable, is just as essential to its subjective effects. In Lacanian accounts, the impossible kernel at the subject's core is formed in a series of gaps. The first is located between the organism and the body. The second is between the body – as the consistency of its enjoyments, as narcissism, as the unsignifiable relation to *jouissance*, as drive, as image, and as gestalt – and the realm of the signifier. We have two gaps, one a sort of mythical beginning, the other being more accessible to symbolic formations and structures.

These gaps emerge because of an inherent incommensurability among the levels of subjective constitution and from the fact that our relationship to the Other is marked by the limits of the signifier. We are inhabited by a language that we learn from those who must give us a reason for being through their desires. This is initially articulated in the exchange where our bodies serve as the first gifts to the Other, our first answer to what it asks: that must give us our being as its return. Conversely, the signifier limits the Other; its meanings are not ultimately readable and extend beyond anyone's intentions. Both grammar and consciousness fail. No Chomsky to the rescue here. No language as a tool here. There is not even a dialogue between two selves negotiating reality. Language is a social practice under-girded by the stakes of transforming the inchoate body into a site of meaning and desire. *It is at this last level that the signifier's effects operate most irrationally within ideological formations such as traditional gender identifications. Thus it is interesting, perhaps a matter of privacy, that this corporeal cusp is not often addressed in acquaintance rape programmes and seldom in theories about sexuality and aggression. Nor do we consider how one ethically acts in relationship to a corporeality that founds the very consciousness that is meant to control it.*

At this level of corporeal inscription, as that inscription functions as an address to the Other, one can re-visit the psychoanalytic notion of the drive. In fact, one can see Freud's notion of the drive as the psychoanalytic effort to speak to the mind/body problem that is so baffling to cognition driven theories.[41] The drive is not an instinct and for Lacanians at least it refers to the Other and to the register of demand. For demand, unlike desire, presumes that there is an object that will resolve the inconstancies and problematic of the address to the Other. Demand presumes the impossible object resides in the Other, not in one's own desire,[42] and the drive emerges not because there ever was such an object but because there never was such an object. It is at this juncture that we can return to the question of *jouissance*.

> We may speak of this limit as a failure of representation, not simply in the abstract sense of a loss of meaning, or even in the sense of an excess of meaning (the fact that there is no closure to the movement of signification), but in the concrete sense that the drive will attempt to compensate for this failure (a lack in the Other) by producing something at the level of bodily jouissance – a jouissance that the subject does not desire.[43]

Here *jouissance* short-circuits the relationship by which sexuality is transformed into human desire. Anyone guilty of telling another person to 'go fuck himself' articulates a sense of sexuality ethically indifferent to the Other's desire. Acting out that indifference is another question but still asks us to elaborate a theory of aggression and sexuality, one that de-constructs the subjective structures that both bind and unravel the meaning of patriarchal privilege. Sex and aggression seem, in part, to follow from impasses in male identity, found in same-sex identification, and in relationship to a sort of repetitious sexual drive. Those more likely to have sexually assaulted a woman masturbate more, have more partners, and are more frequently aroused.[44] They also report that they are more sexually dissatisfied. Should we simply dichotomise power and sexuality or resolve the problem in the way that Craig Palmer's counter-feminist essay on rape does by relegating both to a biological pre-given.[45] In one case the sexual as embodied is divorced from power as political. In the other, we have a reactionary justification that erases men's subjective responsibility.

Drives always involve a mis-recognition of the Other/other. Rape is an aggressive act with the odd provision that the victim is supposed to enjoy the violation. Such mis-perceived enjoyment is found in the case of convicted stranger-rape perpetrators, in acquaintance rapists and can be deduced from the reactions of 'normal' men to certain sexual scenarios.[46] Rapists often see themselves as innocent, led on, and often those who rape in a dating situation will ask the woman out again.[47] A number of convicted rapists see themselves as making *her* fantasy come true.[48] Traditional gender roles and rape myths ascribe a sexual aggressiveness to the male that is needed to free a woman to experience *jouissance*.[49]

I am suggesting that the current alliance between the political and psychology in the arena of sexual aggression leaves an important theoretical dimension unthought. Without reflection on subjectivity, the psychological, especially at the level of intervention, will return to its usual formations. The political axis, stripped of either an institutional or psychological referent, will be absorbed into a liberal approach. The dimension of the subjective allows another perspective on rape prevention, one that retains its radical relation to the social link, the formation of gender, and the non-rationality of desire and the drive.

Strategies of prevention

Since it is mostly men who rape, it is obvious that one answer to the question of rape resides in patriarchal entitlement. Women are like property or subordinates whom men have the right to enjoy as they please. Rape keeps women in their place. This argument is forcefully presented by Susan Brownmiller, Andrea Dworkin, and many others.[50] Since rapists are more likely to believe rape myths and believe in traditional gender configurations, it is also obvious that certain social discourses affect rape rates. Cross-cultural research on gender and rape confirms the influence of the social status of the sexes and further indicates that differential economic resources often play a role.[51] Following these paths of research, encouraging reflections on patriarchal beliefs is a primary aim of a number of interventions in acquaintance rape prevention.

In contrast to problematic traditional gender roles, prevention discourses offer a model of sexual equality where agreement and consent replace asymmetrical models of heterosexual interactions. Prevention programmes also give men and women a clearer sense of the legal sanctions that are in place with respect to rape. Some research although not all has found that these sorts of prevention programmes appear to change men's attitudes in relation to rape and gender at least temporarily. Women's views, which are not far from the ideals and perspectives endorsed by the programme, undergo less change.[52]

The 'miscommunication' model of rape prevention also plays a prominent role in prevention programmes. In this model, it is proposed that rape occurs because the parties, two equal partners, do not communicate with sufficient clarity. The parties are presumed to share parallel responsibilities for communication. However, any careful textual or protocol analysis reveals that it is the women who bear the burden of clear communication. It is assumed that the man communicates perfectly his desires. This model also ushers in somewhat different models of sexuality and seduction.

> To us consent is the continual process of explicit, verbal discussion, a
> dialogue, brief or extended, taken one step at a time, to an expressed 'yes'
> by both parties and a shared acknowledgement that at this moment what
> we are doing together is safe and comfortable to each of us.[53]

In critique of such approaches, Mary Crawford brings up a study in which the miscommunication model is compared to a traditional gender model as grids for understanding the causes of rape.[54] Men, but not women, perceive the woman as more culpable when exposed to the miscommunication model than when exposed to a model of sexual relationships in which men are dominant but also responsible. In terms of the ideas of this paper, the communication model, even when it is accompanied by assertiveness training for women, assumes a given form of subjectivity. This subject is transparent to itself, knows what it wants, and possesses a certain relationship between its being and its words as opposed to existing as a certain relationship between its being and its words. Let's call that subject the expressive humanistic subject. *This subject is the social constructionist subject turned on its head; the road between signifiers, identities, and desire is clear and uncomplicated.*

As an alternative to the communication model, one could invoke instead an ethics of the limit rather than the ethics of agreement. Certainly women have been burdened with being the gatekeepers of sexuality. However, they have functioned in this role, at least since the sexual revolution, without any authority, or traditionally as in the safe-keeping of men. An ethics of the Other has been collapsed into endless dyads of communicating individuals, and limit in the West is often not read as a question of ethics, subjective responsibility, restraint, but rather as a matter of deprivation. Limit is not popular in late capitalism, especially a limit on one's enjoyment.

Moreover, if we are to rely on super-ordinate subjects of communication as our theory of subjectivity, I need to understand if those subjects are gendered or if gender is an accidental feature of their desires and the signifiers that found those desires. Does this subject experience anything like the drive between its mind and body? These remarks are not meant to vitiate the importance of these programmes for improving the quality of life of women and of heterosexual relationships. I am only saying that the theorisation of subjectivity is currently incomplete and thus that the programme may be insufficiently radical. I would make the same argument for those theories of acquaintance rape that see subjectivity solely as forms of resistance to persuasion (admittedly we see the Lacanian idea of the subject as an effect of the Other, but in a rather degraded form).

Those prevention approaches that apply certain feminist insights to transform North America's rape culture in principle take gender to its limit as the earlier quotation from Capraro suggests. For its part, this strategy necessarily asks us to fully interrogate what constitutes gender and its relation to sexual drives. Such an inquiry is requisite to our assuming that sexuality and the dynamics of rape bear no relation to one another, that rape is solely about power. This is an important consideration for those exploring rape prevention.[55] If there is another dimension, another way power is imbricated in gender and sexuality, one could expand one's understanding of patriarchy and its social transformation.

Patriarchy may bear a relation to sexuality through the impasses that are generated in gaps that define the entrance of our bodies into the logic of the signifier. As a relationship to the signifier, one could not simply assume that things would run smoothly. Norms, including patriarchal ones, cover this failure. Sexuality inhabits this gap, as the 'cause' of desire and/or the drive. As an implication, could there be more than one structural form to the difficulties that define the human body and does 'doing' gender have any relation to lacks and sutures that emerge between body and signifier? The answer could be no. But it might be yes. The point is that so few in psychology even consider these questions. Nor do we consider how pursuing them can encourage subjective responsibility and ground-ethical action.

> From a Lacanian perspective, biological definitions of gender assume that the Other (sex) is both embodied and extant – while theories of 'socially constructed gender' assume that the Other exists but is not embodied. Lacan's point is quite different: the Other is embodied but the fact that the Other has a body does not mean, *of necessity*, that the Other exists.[56]

Metzger is getting at the failure and gaps that mark the Other in the body. It is possible then that we would learn as much from sexual failures, from hate as well as love, what impossibilities and structures we must encounter in emancipating sexual desire from aggression and victimisation. It is also from this place that we can further transform the forms of repression and oppression of which ideologies of sexuality and gender are the mark.

Collaboration

This paper invites a certain work of dialogue and asks for certain sorts of collaborations. Outside of North America, ideas from Lacanian psychoanalysis are integrated into clinical and social programmes.

Within these contexts, questions of the 'Other' and various Lacanian concepts are integrated within a daily praxis instead of being academic esoteria. In the main, in Anglophone countries, the Lacanian framework and feminist interests are joined in cultural studies and literature. But, psychoanalysis and feminism are both founded in a praxis of transformation. The circumscription of Lacanian psychoanalysis to the university and of other psychoanalytic feminisms to social *theory* and clinical circles (at least this is my reading of the scene in the United States) leaves a whole field of social interventions to what I have argued are limited ideas of human freedom, desire, identity, and transformation. It is very important to understand how the intersection of the body and culture functions to produce desiring beings. Otherwise one's efforts may have a limited effect, as seen here in the follow-up results of present acquaintance rape efforts, or one may replicate particular ideological effects (psychology's usual notion of the self) without any particular reflection on that decision. I see this task as parallel to a heightened awareness of the production of subject positions and as comparable to other social and political re-formulations of psychology, such as increased cultural sensitivity to marginalised populations and cultural context. But it is not the job of theory alone; it requires a truly innovative collaboration aimed toward intervention.

Notes

1. According to Bechhofer and Parrot the first research paper on sexual violence appeared in 1957, L. Bechhofer and A. Parrot, 'What is Acquaintance Rape', in A. Parrot and L. Bechhofer (eds), *Acquaintance Rape: The Hidden Crime*, John Wiley & Sons, New York 1991, pp9-25.
2. M. Koss, 'Hidden Rape: Sexual Aggression and Victimisation in a National Sample of Students in Higher Education', in P. Searles and R. Berger (eds), *Rape and Society*, Westview Press, Boulder 1995, pp35-49.
3. *Ibid.*
4. J. L. Hermann, 'Considering Sex Offenders: A Model of Addiction', in P. Searles, and R. Berger (eds), *Rape and Society, op. cit.*, pp75-95.
5. H. Pinzone-Glover, C. Gidycz and C. Jacobs, 'An Acquaintance Rape Prevention Program', *Psychology of Women Quarterly*, 22, 1998, pp605-622.
6. There is some debate about whether research and intervention into acquaintance rape is too closely tied to women on college campuses and to dating, and might not also need to expand to other social settings and become more inclusive in its research. Prevalence data is varied and the indifference to poor women not unexpected. See: P. Reid, 'Poor Women in Psychological Research: Shut-up and Shut out', *Psychology of Women*

Quarterly, 17, 1993, pp133-150; Pinzone-Glover et al., *op. cit.*; L. Bourque, *Defining Rape*, Duke University Press, Durham, NC 1989.

7. See, for example, A. Berkowitz, 'A model acquaintance rape prevention programme for men', in A. Berkowitz (ed), *Men and Rape: Theory, Research, and Prevention Programs in Higher Education*, Jossey Bass, San Francisco 1994, pp35-42.

8. For a different view see P. Anderson and C. Struckman-Johnson, *Sexually Aggressive Women: Current Perspectives and Controversies*, The Guilford Press, New York 1998.

9. Cited in K. Lonsway, 'Preventing Acquaintance Rape Through Education: What do we Know?', *Psychology of Women Quarterly*, 20, 1996, pp229-266.

10. A. Berkowitz, *op. cit.*

11. M. Heppner, H. Neville, K. Smith, D. Kivlighan and B. Gershuny, 'Examining Immediate and Long Term Efficacy of Rape Prevention Programming with Racially Diverse College Men', *Journal of Counselling Psychology*, 46, 1999, pp16-26.

12. K. Hanson and C. Gidyez, 'Evaluation of a Sexual Assault Program', *Journal of Counselling and Clinical Psychology*, 61, 1993, pp1046-1052.

13. K. Drieschner and Lange, 'A Review of Cognitive Factors in the Etiology of Rape: Theories, Empirical Studies, and Implications', *Clinical Psychology Review*, 19, 1999, pp57-77; K. Lonsway, *op. cit.*

14. Feminist Legal Theory which draws from MacKinnon to Drucilla Cornell.

15. P. Donat and J. D'Emilio, 'A Feminist Re-definition of Rape and Sexual Aggression: Historical Foundations and Change', in M.E. Ogden and J. Clay-Warner (eds), *Confronting Rape and Sexual Assault*, SR Books: Worlds of Women, Wilmington, Delaware, #3, 1998, pp35-50.

16. See the discussion over politics and rape research in recent issues of the *American Psychologist*; G. Nagayama Hall and C. Barongan, 'Prevention of Sexual Aggression: Socio-cultural Risk and Protective Factors', *American Psychologist*, 52, 1997, pp5-14; G. E. Zuriff, 'Ideology over reason', *American Psychologist*, 54, 1999, p71.

17. R. Capraro, 'Disconnected Lives: Men, Masculinity, and Rape Prevention', in A. Berkowitz (ed), *Men and Rape: Theory, Research, and Prevention Programs in Higher Education*, Jossey Bass, San Francisco 1994, p22.

18. S. Wilkinson (ed), *Feminist Social Psychologies*, Open University Press, London 1996, p5.

19. M. Heppner at al., *op. cit.*; K. Lonsway, *op. cit.*

20. See J. Prouix, A. McKibben and R. Lusigan, 'Relationships Between Affective Components and Sexual Behaviours in Sexual Aggressors', *Sexual Abuse: A Journal of Research and Treatment*, 8, 1996, pp279-289.

21. P. Anderson and C. Struckman-Johnson, *op. cit.*

22. R. Nisbett and T. Wilson, 'Telling More Than We Can Know: Verbal Reports on Mental Processes', *Psychological Review*, 84, 1977, pp250-256.

23. de Lauretis, cited in P. Elliot, *From Mastery to Analysis*, Cornell University Press, Ithaca, NY 1991, p24.

24. Wilson, cited in L. Segal, 'Feminism in Psychoanalysis', *new formations*, 28, 1996, pp85-100; R. Bowlby, 'Still Crazy After All These Years', in T. Brennan (ed), *Between Psychoanalysis and Feminism*, Routledge, New York 1989, pp40-60.

25. Benecke, 1995; D. Scully and J. Marolla, 'Riding the Bull at Gilley's: Convicted Rapists Describe the Rewards of Rape', in P. Searles and R. Berger (eds), *Rape and Society*, *op.cit.*, pp58-73.

26. Dreischner and Lange, *op. cit.*, 1999.

27. L. Bourque, *op. cit.*

28. See R. Salecl, *(Per)versions of Love and Hate*, Verso, London 1998.

29. Dreischner and Lange, *op. cit.*, 1999.

30. A. Fausto-Sterling, *Myths of Gender*, Basic Books, New York 1985.

31. See Dreischner and Lange, 1999; J. Prouix, A. McKibbon, and R. Lusignan, *op. cit.*

32. N. Chodorow, *Feminism and Psychoanalytic Theory*, Yale University Press, New Haven, CT 1989, p8.

33. A. Hurtado, 'Relating to Privilege: Seduction & Rejection in the Subordination of White Women and Women of Color', *Signs*, 14, 1989, pp883-895.

34. E. Cowie, 'Pornography and Fantasy: Psychoanalytic Perspectives', in L. Segal, and M. McIntosh (eds), *Sex Exposed*, Rutgers, New Brunswick 1993.

35. Robin Warshaw, *I Never Called it Rape*, Harper and Rowe, New York 1998.

36. L. Hengehold, 'Between Rape and Desired Sex: Making a More Complex Difference', *Journal for the Psychoanalysis of Culture and Society*, 3, 1998, pp27-40.

37. J. Bargh, P. Raymond, J. Pryor and F. Strack, 'Attractiveness of the Underling: An Automatic Power – Sex Association and its Consequences for Sexual Harassment and Aggression', *Journal of Personality and Social Psychology*, 68, 1995, pp768-781.

38. C. Mackinnon, *Feminism Unmodified*, Harvard University Press, Cambridge, MA 1987.

39. J. D. Nasio, 'Five Lessons on the Psychoanalytic Theory of Jacques Lacan', D. Pettigrew and F. Raffoul (trans), State University Press of New York, Albany, NY 1992/1998.

40. J. Gurewich, 'Toward a New Alliance between Psychoanalysis and Social Theory', in D. Pettigrew, and F. Raffoul (eds), *Disseminating Lacan*, SUNY Press, Albany 1996.

41. R. Grigg, 'Dualism and the Drives', *Umbr(a)*, 1, 1997, pp159-165.

42. P. Hill, *Lacan for beginners*, Writers and Readers Ltd., London 1997.

43. C. Shepardson, 'The Gift of Love, the Debt of Desire', *Differences*, 10, 1998, pp30-74.

44. L. Bourque, *op. cit.*

45. C. Palmer, 'Twelve Reasons why Rape is not Sexually Motivated: A Sceptical Examination', *Journal of Sex Research*, 25, 1988, pp512-530.

46. Donnerstein and Linz, 'Mass Media Sexual Violence, and Male Viewers',

in M. E. Ogden, and J. Clay-Warner (eds), *Confronting Rape and Sexual Assault*, SR Books: Worlds of Women, Wilmington, Delaware, #3, 1998, pp181-198.

47. Koss, *op. cit.*

48. See D. Scully and J. Marolla, *op. cit.*, p112.

49. M. Burt, 'Rape Myths', in M. E. Ogden, and J. Clay-Warner (eds), *Confronting Rape and Sexual Assault*, *op. cit.*, pp129-144.

50. S. Brownmiller, *Against our Will*, Fawcett Columbine, New York 1975; A. Dworkin, 'I Want a Twenty-four Hour Truce During Which There is no Rape', in E. Buchwald, P. Fletcher and M. Roth (eds), *Transforming a Rape Culture*, Milkweed Editions, Minneapolis, MN 1993, pp11-22.

51. P. Sanday, 'Rape and the Silencing of the Feminine', in S. Tomaselli and R. Porter (eds), *Rape*, Basil Blackwell, Oxford 1986, pp84-101.

52. H. Pinzone-Glover, C. Gidycz, and C. Jacobs, *op. cit.*

53. J. Weinberg and M. Biernbaum, 'Conversations of Consent: Sexual Intimacy Without Sexual Assault', in E. Buchwald, P. Fletcher and M. Roth (eds), *Transforming a Rape Culture*, *op. cit.*, p 93.

54. M. Crawford, 'Date Rape: The Social Construction of Miscommunication', Paper presentation at American Psychological Association, New York, August 1995.

55. See Hermann, *op. cit.*

56. D. Metzger, 'Sexuation and the Drives', *Umbr(a)* 1, 1997, p94.

An approach to synchronicity: from synchrony to synchronisation

Benjamin Sylvester Bradley

Such phenomena of synchronicity as telepathy, oracles and clairvoyance stand beyond the pale of individualistic psychologies. Here I argue that synchronicity is only susceptible to understandings that recognise a collective basis for mentation, a view familiar to most critical psychologists. My approach is drawn from Saussure's analysis of speech as primarily organised along a synchronic dimension and from an idea of synchronisation implicit in Althusser's analysis of social reproduction. I note that Saussurean synchrony implies that what is physically and/or temporally absent is intrinsic to the experience of 'presence.' From here I develop a notion of psychical synchronisation as something inevitably affording synchronicities. I end by showing that what would have to be added to my analysis if it were to cover all cases of synchronicity is a co-ordination between the psychical and the material as is implicit in what physicists attempt to theorise as a 'unified field'.

There is no science of the subject. Any thought mastering the subject is mystical.[1]

One thing common to the otherwise diverse movement of critical psychology is the attempt to re-work the consequences of individualism for the study of Psyche. Some talk of social construction, others of deconstruction, logocentrism or relational forms, yet others of dialogue or intertextuality, narrative or discourse. But all agree that, whatever we understand to be the mind, that understanding is collectively produced. By this may be meant only that any talk about the subject-matter of psychology is regulated by the same processes of making significance that sustain all language. In this case, the very idea of 'subjectivity' and the psychical may be held an epiphenomenon of discourse, 'neither required nor demanded by "what there is"'.[2]

Alternatively, we can accept with Giddens that cultural systems have a duality which simultaneously consists in those rules and regulations that constitute social structure *and* the knowledge-laden subjectivities of the situated actors who draw upon these rules and regulations in reproducing such systems in their interactions.[3] In this case, if the subjective domain of society is collectively produced and reproduced, its psychical dynamics too will be supra-individual. Viewed thus, we may be less puzzled by a small child's quickness to catch the sense of what someone they have never met before is saying than if we assume sense-making is something each individual must separately produce for themselves. The two speakers have simply accessed the same deep metaphors of discourse so that they know, quite literally, where the other 'is coming from'.[4]

We do not have to go much further down this line of reasoning before we are in a position to re-visit a whole host of phenomena which have hitherto seemed inexplicable or marginal to individualistic psychology. In this, I believe, we see a significant strength of critical psychology: that it provides grounds for taking seriously topics that previous psychologies have been content to put in the too-hard bin. For it is an old principle of deconstruction that, when discussing knowledge claims such as those made by psychologists, we must seek in the shadows for the key to the dynamics which determine what stands in the light.[5] There is perhaps no part of the psychic domain more fully eclipsed in psychological discussion, or marginalised as unverifiable or anomalous, than the one I deal with here: synchronicity.[6] In asking what psychology would have to be like in order to take the topic of synchronicity seriously, I argue that the changes required have implications that go far beyond that topic itself.

Examples of synchronicity

Synchronicity is one of those topics of research with which everyone seems keen to help, from close friends to the faintest acquaintance. Before I discuss the definition of synchronicity, I will list a few examples of the kinds of evidence that people cite in illustration of the phenomenon:

(a) The Sunday afternoon before attending the conference at which I gave the first version of this paper, I drove into Sydney to a prior meeting. I returned home on Wednesday to finish my talk. One of the e-mail messages I found waiting for me was a reply to a friendly message I had shot off at 16.11pm just before I left for Sydney the previous Sunday:

> Sunday, April 25 1999, 16.58pm. Well, my dear Ben, I turned on the email specifically to write you a brief note and yours is the single new message I received!

My correspondent, Sean, was a man I had met a year previously at a small week-long Leicester-style 'working conference'. Since that time we have both been involved in a virtual group, a continuation of the conference by e-mail. Over the year, both Sean and I had contributed many messages to the group *qua* group – and at least once disagreed quite vehemently in messages sent to the group as a whole. But before this Sunday, I had never sent him a personal e-mail message 'out of the blue.' Neither had he sent me such a message. Yet, during 4 and 5pm that Sunday afternoon, at a time when I had the need to illustrate synchronicity on my mind, we both had the impulse to send each other private messages.

(b) Witchcraft and sorcery. Evans-Pritchard gives an eye-witness account of witchcraft: an inexplicable light smoothly moving towards a remote hut in Zandeland which, as morning showed, then suffered misadventure.[7] Similar examples of sorcery are to be heard of in Australia's remote aboriginal and islander communities.

(c) Oracles (such as the Tarot pack and palmistry). Thus Jung, writing of the Chinese oracle, the *I Ching*, which interprets the results of the micro-physical event of tossing coins in the air (or dividing yarrow stalks), assumes 'the coincidence of events in space and time as meaning something more than mere chance, namely, a peculiar interdependence of objective events among themselves as well as with the subjective (psychic) states of the observer or observers.' In this 'the ancient Chinese mind contemplates the cosmos in a way comparable to that of the modern physicist, who cannot deny that his [or her] model of the world is a decidedly psychophysical structure ... the physical events A' and B' are of the same quality as the psychic events C' and D' ... all are exponents of one and the same momentary situation'.[8]

(d) Astrology. The Gauquelins' research suggests that there is a statistically significant relationship between the rising signs (the planet rising at the time of birth) of great achievers and the area of their achievement (for instance Mars and military achievement). This research is hard to fault in the view of Eysenck and Nias.[9]

(e) Cases of mediumship of the kind evinced by Mrs Piper in William James' observations of her seances. James argues that her knowledge about the secret love-affair and financial dealings of the dead psychologist Hodgson were neither easily explicable, nor trivial, nor fraudulent. While he was unable to accept the 'strong' hypothesis that Hodgson had a spiritual existence after death, James proposed that Mrs Piper must have picked up these details through an unconscious process of thought-transference, either directly, during Hodgson's life, or via James after Hodgson's death. Summing up his work as a 'psychical researcher,' James wrote:

> Out of my experience [with psychical research] one fixed conclusion dogmatically emerges, and that is this, that we with our lives are like islands in the sea, or like trees in the forest ... The trees ... commingle their roots in the darkness underground, and the islands also hang together through the ocean's bottom. Just so there is a continuum of cosmic consciousness against which our individuality builds but accidental fences, and into which our several minds plunge as into a mother-sea or reservoir.[10]

(h) Some of the strongest evidence for telepathy or thought-transfer comes in psycho-analysis. Both Freud and later analysts have published examples.[11]

(i) Further evidence comes from the Ganzfeld and other experiments published in serials like the *Journal of Parapsychology*.[12] One of particular interest is by Schlitz and LaBerge.[13] They seated experimental subjects two by two in two different rooms, well separated physically but connected by closed-circuit television. A camera was permanently 'on' in one room, and directed at the first subject. In the other room, the second subject viewed a monitor which was randomly switched 'on' and 'off.' When it was 'on' s/he saw the first subject. Subsequent analysis showed that the periods during which the monitor was switched 'on' coincided with significantly higher levels of skin conductance in the subjects who were being observed than when the monitor was 'off,' even though they could not tell when they were being observed.

Jung's definition of synchronicity

If the discussion of 'synchronicity' has a history in psychology, then most would treat Carl Jung's volume of that name, published in 1952, as one of its way-stations. Jung's book defines synchronicity as 'the simultaneous occurrence of a certain psychic state with one or more external events which appear as meaningful parallels to the momentary subjective state'.[14]

But he illustrates it with a study that shows the identification of synchronicity with simultaneity to be problematic. The bulk of his evidence comes from the analysis of the horoscopes of four hundred married couples (especially, conjunctions between the moon in the woman's horoscope and the sun in the man's). But whatever we think of Jung's mathematics, his data can, at best, only point to a relationship of something that happened in the distant past, in the sky at the times of the lovers' births, with their attraction to each other now. Synchronicity may involve a greater or lesser time-lag between the events it connects. And this, as we shall see, is an important clue to defining synchronicity. For it suggests that synchronicity as Jung defines it can be conceived within the framework of synchrony as Saussure defines it.

From synchronicity to synchrony

Saussure as psychologist

When we are taught the history of psychology, Ferdinand de Saussure is unlikely to be mentioned, unless it be as a linguist. Yet Saussure described himself as a psychologist and his work proves relevant to the psychology of synchronicity for more than one reason. For instance: Saussure argued that linguistics, insofar as it dealt with language as a system of signs and not as a collection of physical speech acts, had something as its object that, like synchronicity, was at once 'purely social and independent of the individual' and 'exclusively psychological'.[15]

Saussure saw linguistics as being in the vanguard of the human science to which it belonged, psychology, in that what was essential to linguistics was also likely to be essential to many other areas of psychological inquiry. In this light, his seminal differentiation of synchronic from diachronic analysis in linguistics was intended as a contribution to psychology in general. He argued that any science concerned with values cannot proceed without making a distinction between the system of values *per se* and the same values as they relate to time. He described language as 'a system of pure values which are determined by nothing except the momentary arrangement of its terms'.[16] Hence his distinction between the two axes of linguistic explanation (see figure 1):

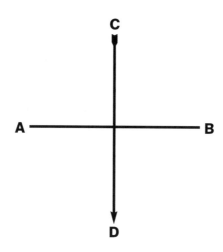

(1) *the axis of simultaneities* (AB), which stands for the relations of coexisiting things and from which the intervention of time is excluded; and

(2) *the axis of successions* (CD), on which only one thing can be considered at a time but upon which are located all the things on the first axis together with their changes (Sassure 1974, p80)

So far as the speaker is concerned, Saussure said, succession in time does not exist. The speaker confronts a state of simultaneity. Hence the linguist can only enter the minds of speakers by completely suppressing the past and knowledge of history. The words a speaker utters must be seen as part of a synchronic system that, in the first instance, must be defined in terms of what the speaker (not the linguist) perceives to be reality. Saussure draws a parallel with chess. In a state of the set of chessmen, the respective value of each piece depends on its position on the chessboard just as each linguistic term derives its value from its opposition to all other terms. Both chess and language are governed by a set of social conventions. And in both chess and language, a single change (for instance the insertion of the word 'not' into a sentence or losing your queen) affects the values of all the elements in the system. Hence, each 'diachronic' move separates a synchronic state entirely from its predecessor:

> In a game of chess any particular position has the unique characteristic of being freed from all antecedent positions; the route used in arriving there makes absolutely no difference; one who has followed the entire course of the match has no advantage over the curious party who comes up at a critical moment to inspect the game; to describe this arrangement, it is perfectly useless to recall what had just happened ten seconds previously. All this is equally applicable to language and sharpens the radical distinction between diachrony and synchrony. Speaking operates only on a language-state, and the changes that intervene between states have no place in either state.[17]

The realm of cause and the realm of meaning are compatible

At this point it is important to remind ourselves that diachronic and synchronic analysis are not incompatible according to Saussure. Both forms of analysis can be applied to the same phenomenon: a move in a chess game, a sentence, or an experience. A full explanation of any psychological event requires both approaches. This point was famously made by Evans-Pritchard in his study of Azande witchcraft when he argued that the diachronic explanation of death by causation and the synchronic or psychic explanation in terms of meaning (witchcraft) answered quite different but compatible questions.[18]

Evans-Pritchard pointed out that the persistence of beliefs in witchcraft, both in complex industrial and smaller-scale societies, shows that modern science cannot address a certain type of question. Suppose, for example, that people live in a culture like Zandeland, where grain is stored in large wooden structures. When the sun gets hot, the Azande will seek shelter in the granary's shade. There is nothing wonderful about that. Every now and then an old granary will collapse, its legs eaten away by termites. There is nothing odd there either. But it follows that occasionally people will be sitting in the shade of the granary when it collapses and be injured or killed as a result. The question is: why were those particular people hurt by the granary's collapse? Science can explain the building's fall. It can explain why people like the cool. But the fact that these two causal sequences overlap is called chance, bad luck, coincidence.

This response cuts no ice with the Azande. It begs their question. So they invoke a form of psychical efficacy, witchcraft, which they test for with oracles (e.g., by interpreting the innards of a ritually-poisoned chicken). They do not deny the claims of science – the action of termites, the need for shelter from the sun. They seek to explain a meaningful coincidence, something beyond the reach of a science that only recognises causal explanation. Superficially, said Evans-Pritchard, witchcraft is an explanation that is cast in a causal form: the reason the man died is because someone had 'pointed a stick' at him. But Evans-Pritchard argued that witchcraft accusations are actually produced collectively, as a form of expression of current inter-personal and inter-group tensions within the Zande community.

This conforms to what Jung said: we should not look for a causal explanation of synchronicities. Synchronicity is 'an a-causal connecting principle'... 'we must conclude that besides the connection between cause and effect there is another factor in nature which expresses itself in the arrangement of events and appears to us as meaning'.[19] There is, Jung says, a 'secret correspondence' between natural events, to be witnessed, for example, in the workings of the Taoist oracle, the *I Ching*.

The primacy of the synchronic in psychological analysis

Here we glimpse the prospect of a different argument, namely, that, despite its current neglect, synchronic analysis should take precedence over diachronic explanation in psychology. I elaborate this elsewhere in a critique of the predominance of diachronic explanation in contemporary psychology.[20] Suffice it to point out here that nearly all psychologists' favourite forms of explanation nowadays are diachronic:

developmental, evolutionary, nature and nurture, biological bases, experimental, causal. Yet, in each of these spheres, there has gathered a considerable stock of evidence that, as in Saussure's linguistics, synchronic analysis is required before one can identify what needs to be explained diachronically.

Synchrony is not raw simultaneity

When Saussure speaks of synchrony, he does not refer literally to events that occur at the same chronological instant. In the same way, synchronicities do not usually occur at exactly the same time. At best, one person does something, phones for example, just as the person they were phoning was preparing to do the same thing. At worst, as in Jung's birth charts, decades may separate the relevant events.[21]

What Saussure means by synchrony has two important aspects here. The first is that, phenomenologically, from the speaker's viewpoint, the 'presence' of the present must be presumed to consist solely in simultaneities: my mother's wrinkled smile, my father's evergreen absence, a bright winter day, Bach on the radio, the latest carnage in Sierra Leone, my aching head, the unsettling sense I have forgotten something; all are my 'here and now,' one simultaneity. The second is more analytic: both language and experience must be readable in a way to which temporal sequence has no immediate relevance. It is in this vein that Saussure develops his argument that the relations and differences between linguistic terms in a language state are structured along two contrasting dimensions (see figure 1).

One is made up by the combination of different kinds of term, terms which are both contiguous and (at least) successively present. Saussure calls this form of organisation 'syntagmatic'. Think of the juxtaposition of different kinds of furniture across the floor of a room: bed, chair, dresser, mirror. Or the layout of a house: porch, hall, lounge, kitchen, bedroom, bathroom. Or the sequence of a meal: aperitif, entrée, main course, dessert, coffee, liqueur. In chess: a pawn threatens a bishop while black's queen checks white's king. Or a sentence: subject, verb, qualifier, object. In each case, the terms gain meaning from the order in which they are strung together, spatial or temporal. Thus a word gains some of its significance from its opposition to everything that comes before or after it in dialogue.

At the same time, signs gain value from the place they have in a set of relations and oppositions from which time is excluded, that is 'paradigmatically' (see A —— B in figure 1). Here meaning is derived by a process of selection from a single set of semantically-related (but different) terms. I select a king-size four-poster bed, not a single trestle. I choose salad, not paté for my entrée. A pawn moves in a different way from a knight. I select the verb 'peer', not 'look'. Paradigmatic series are tied together by varying degrees of opposition. This is the domain of antonyms and synonyms. It is also the domain of metaphor, and is often personally idiosyncratic, as related terms evoke each other by association.[22]

Saussure observes that syntagmatic relations occur 'in praesentia' whereas paradigmatic relations occur 'in absentia in a potential mnemonic series'.[23] A synchronic language-state includes both what is present and what might have been present but is absent, being instead actually or potentially 'in the memory'. In James' words, the present 'can never be a fact of our immediate experience':[24] 'Le moment ou je parle est déjà loin de moi'.[25] But this obvious point masks a subtle one. The present always means more to the individual who experiences it than is ever 'there' in the data available to the senses. Vision, for example, is 'ill-posed' in formal terms: there is never sufficient information in the retinal image uniquely to determine the visual scene. Hence, 'the brain must make certain assumptions about the real world to resolve this ambiguity, and visual illusions can result when these assumptions are invalid'.[26]

Hence, what I take to be the visible, audible, tangible present is what it is by virtue of events and meanings that are far distant from this 'now' in space and time but, in my idiosyncratic sensibility and experience, can be related to it. This is where we come close to certain phenomena of synchronicity: where *what is observably present (and so scientifically 'knowable') is semantically connected to what is empirically absent (i.e. 'unknowable')*. And, given that, synchronically, any thing's meaning depends less on simultaneity than on its paradigmatic and syntagmatic differences from other elements in the system of which it forms part – or as Saussure puts it, 'in language there are only differences'[27], anomaly surrounds a case where two elements in the system seem the same or are very difficult to differentiate: sameness becomes anomalous. These meaningful anomalies are what we call synchronicities.

Banal synchronicity

I now want to introduce the idea that synchronicity is, in one regard, perfectly banal. That is, from a socio-political perspective, modern society is nothing but a great engine for producing synchronicities.[28]

Althusser furnished us with an introduction to this idea when he took up the problem of the necessity for the reproduction of the relations of labour power from Quesnay and Marx. He described the parallel problem of the reproduction of the material conditions of production as follows:

> Mr X, a capitalist who produces woollen yarn in his spinning-mill, has to 'reproduce' his raw material, his machines, etc. But *he* does not produce them for his own production – other capitalists do: an Australian sheep-farmer, Mr Y, a heavy engineer producing machine-tools, Mr Z, etc. etc. And Mr Y and Mr Z, in order to produce those products which are the conditions of the reproduction of Mr X's conditions of production, also have to reproduce the conditions of their own production, and so on to infinity – the whole in proportions such that, on the national and even the world market, the demand for means of production (of reproduction) can be satisfied by the supply.[29]

The same goes, *mutatis mutandis*, for the reproduction of the relations that constitute the labour force. Subjects have every day to be reproduced in a form such that they readily submit to their subjection to the relations upon which production draws. This is the work of 'ideology existing in a material ideological apparatus,' such as the educational apparatus, the family, the mass media, the law, the arts, religion. These prescribe 'material practices governed by material ritual, which practices exist in the material actions of a subject acting in all consciousness according to his [or her] belief'.[30] This is how 'the attitudes of the individual-subjects' come to fit 'the posts which the socio-technical division of labour assigns to them in production, exploitation, repression, ideologisation, scientific practice etc.'.[31] And fitted with an obviousness that defies comment and transcends history. Hence ideology appears 'eternal'.

A corollary of Althusser's analysis is that consciousness does not have one centre that wholly determines it.[32] Generalising to all situations Lenin's analysis of the Russian revolution as an exceptional time when all ideological and material contradictions coincided, Althusser argues that, if we are to understand the impact of ideological state apparatuses on consciousness and action, we must recognise that all such action is **over**-*determined* by many levels and instances of the social formation. Many social practices/ meaning-systems bear on or serve to give sense to a 'single' event. In short, human subjects are 'created through the incorporation, through the medium of signs' of children and adults into the many overlapping signifying practices which reproduce embodied everyday life.[33] The fact that these social practices are not all of a piece or even contradictory accounts for the fact that the same individual may simultaneously occupy a plurality of subject-positions or be 'multi-subjective'.[34]

This is to say that any gathering of individuals is diversely significant through being socially reproduced. Whether we are clocking on, held up in a traffic jam, going to the pub, dancing at a club, turning on the news, eating with our family, buying clothes, falling in love, or going to the symposium on 'Embodiment and Spirituality' at the Millennium Conference in Sydney, it is because we have been diversely filtered by the sign-systems of ideology, picked out, hailed, pointed in the right direction: semantically *synchronised*.

Psychic synchronisation

So, to say that society reproduces its labour relations is by no means the end of the story. Society synchronises us 'semantically' too. Synchronisation involves what Althusser called the 'relatively autonomous' domain of consciousness. It has a psychical dynamic.

Psychic synchronisation can only be emphasised by the fact that, at a behavioural level, humans (and animals) are equipped with a capacity for the micro-social synchronisation of behaviour from birth. Witness our capacity for learning, for ritualisation, conversational co-ordination, or for the kind of intense 'inter-subjective' sensitivity to expressive attunement which Trevarthen and others have demonstrated in even very young babies.[35]

Such capacities presumably underpin the unconscious transmission of 'basic assumptions' that Bion finds to structure the experience of groups.[36] Interestingly, he links these assumptions to some of the same State Apparatuses that Althusser finds to reproduce social life: dependence (church, school); flight-fight (the Armed Forces); and pairing (popular romantic culture). Bion observed that participants (including himself) in the therapeutic groups that he began to run during the Second World War would often get caught up in dynamics that interfered with the task of the group. For example, he repeatedly found himself drawn to responding to the group's passivity by filling its silences with helpful interpretations which, for all his efforts, seemed to have little effect. Eventually he recognised this as evidence of an unspoken assumption of dependency in the group: he was being expected to solve the members problems solo, without any real effort from them. Alternatively, he or others might become the target for attacks on the very idea that a therapeutic group run in the 'leaderless' way that Bion seemed to prefer could ever solve anyone's problems (the 'fight' assumption). Or he might find the whole group, including himself, would veer constantly towards discussing events or ideas that had nothing to do with the members' needs for therapy, simultaneously acting deaf to any member's attempts to get 'back on track' (the 'flight' assumption). Trying to explain these observations, Bion proposed that human beings share some basic defence-mechanisms which group processes can unconsciously co-ordinate and exploit.[37]

A related form of psychical synchronisation occurs in families. Even from before birth, babies are 'type-cast' in terms of the expectations their parents and other family members have of them. Gender expectations are a case in point,[38] but also far more specific expectations deriving from parents' own histories of attachment, the life-events and characters of older children in the family or previous miscarriages experienced by the mother. After birth, the type-casting can be witnessed in parental baby-talk, mother-baby groups and talk about a child to third parties (gossip).[39] The processes of what Zinner and Shapiro in their observations of adolescents call projective identification and delineation reproduce the family-system in a way that means individual members soon have only a limited range of recognised subject-positions available to them.[40] The key point here is that these systemic processes synchronise the whole family to view individual members in the same way. One example is given by Strouse, who illustrates how Alice James was positioned in the same teasing, seductive, self-centred way by both her father and her oldest brother, William, circumscribing her place in the family as one she could only maintain against stiff competition from idealised other women.[41]

Beyond the family is the work-place, where, once again, a collective process of positioning individuals subjectively is easy to observe. Some are placed as trouble-makers or 'difficult'. Others are seen as slackers, fools, young hopes, caring or uncaring, leadership material, good bosses, bad bosses, stand-offish, sociable, blow-ins, deadwood, team players. Both inside and outside the work-place are fashions, sub-cultures and ritual.[42] These forms of positioning may be unwitting. More conscious processes of psychical synchronisation are to be witnessed in the huge and detailed efforts that go into reproducing Roman Catholics' identification with Christ's passion at Easter. Ideally, individual Catholics go to the same masses week after week, hear and do the same readings, pray for the same causes, prepare themselves for Lent in the same way, go to confession with the same priests, and, during mass, sing, greet, genuflect, cross themselves, pray, listen, sit, stand, kneel, all in unison. Seriously entered into, such ritual can produce extremely powerful collective emotions.

Time-affordances

The idea of synchronisation suggests that one can be out of sync or in sync with others: subject to 'good' or 'bad' timing.[43] This means that social events have a temporal grain which one can either match or flout. And, to the extent that each social situation is over-determined by different discourses, there is no quick way to know what forms of synchronisation any setting affords. Clearly, no one individual is likely to be aware of all the different ways that a given situation socially and psychically signifies. On the other hand, precisely because every social setting has been somewhat synchronised in multiple ways, there is, given opportunity for more perfect calibration, ample potential for synchronicity (viz. the production of anomalous sameness). That is to say that what Walkerdine illustrated as the nascent 'metaphors,' which can be called up from the socially- and psychically-organised discursive practices bearing on any given interpersonal exchange,[44] may synchronously create what Bohm called an 'implicate order' of possible interconnectedness lying behind what is explicit or observable in that exchange.[45]

The question arises therefore of how participants in a social setting might block or facilitate the psychical synchronisation of the metaphorical resources implicit in a given social situation. Here we must recognise a distinction between what a setting affords and how blindly or knowingly, loyally or disloyally, conformingly or subversively we reproduce or repeat it.[46] For no amount of reflection or conscious seeking-out of connectedness can produce synchronicity. Synchronicity is something that arises prior to reflection. It is the grain of experience that one reflects upon. Consciousness is a 'turning back' of experience on itself, a folding of the hitherto unfolded psychic field.[47] Hence, when we are talking about the genesis of synchronicity, we are talking about altering how we co-ordinate the field of experience by varying the production of the specious present and the 'absences' or differences which Saussure argued in order to give it sense.

At this point a broad spectrum of literature becomes relevant to our discussion. Because if experience has a variety of temporal grains, then, when we wish more acutely to calibrate and reap the synchronicities a setting affords, we must preface communion by the form of attention likely to attune ourselves to those grains. This is, as argued by educators like Freire, a twofold process,[48] for some kinds of social situation, by their very structure, preclude active listening or reciprocal intersubjectivity on behalf of some or all participants. This is true of what Freire called monologue, where a single expert, who is set up as the one who is supposed to know, speaks uninterruptedly, scarcely attending to their silenced and pacified audience but only to what he or she has in their own notes/mind.[49] The audience meanwhile is expected dependently to listen.[50] Freire contrasted monologue to dialogue in a social situation approaching what Habermas called an ideal speech situation.[51] This is where there is equality for each participant to gain access to the floor, where there is enough time for any relevant topic to be raised and properly discussed, and where there is freedom for criticism and a full range of self-presentations.

Structuring social conditions is only half the task however. For structure implies agency,[52] the quality of individuals' own subjective engagement in what goes on. It is quite possible to set up the conditions for dialogue, then find no dialogue occurs. This may be because monologically-trained, diachronically-prioritising intellects need to engage in exercises specifically aimed to illuminate the connectedness between our biographies[53] and experiences.[54] Phrased more subjectively, dialogue may fail because participants bring to a situation an 'irritable grasping after fact and reason' where there should be a preparedness to dwell amongst uncertainties and mysteries in what the poet Keats called 'negative capability'.[55] It is along this path that we will become aware of the implications for us as individuals of the paradigmatic, metaphorical resources upon which our current situation draws. These implications are what, according to Volshinov, generate the 'inner speech'[56] which comprises each individual's mental life and by which they must be swayed if they are to become part of the larger conversation of possibilities which their circumstances afford.

There is a notable confluence here. For a host of writers from many different traditions have tried to capture the state of alert surrender that Keats dubbed negative capability. Some talk of tolerance of uncertainty.[57] Others describe the importance of being able just 'to be' in the creative between-space that is neither self nor other.[58] Devereux talks of a need for the behavioural scientist to tolerate counter-transferential disturbances in oneself that are created both by one's own anxieties about being observed by others and by the other's apparently private subjective processes.[59] Levinas talks of a need to recognise the infinitude of the other and the inexplicability of any contact with them.[60] Spiritual writers, particularly those who embrace Eastern and mystical religion, argue that negative capability requires considerable preparation, both physical and mental. For example, Ross writes that, in yoga and meditation, consciousness must free itself from the constraints of the senses so that what is classically known as extra-sensory perception can come into play.[61] And Jaworski, describing what makes a successful leader, contrasts the kind of commitment 'where you seize fate by the throat and do whatever it takes to succeed' with a deeper vision. Here:

> we begin to listen to the inner voice that helps guide us as our journey unfolds. The underlying component of this kind of commitment is our trust in the playing out of our destiny. We have the integrity to stand in a 'state of surrender' ... , knowing that whatever we need at the moment to meet our destiny will be available to us ... We see ourselves as an essential part of the unfolding of the universe ... [Do this and you will then find that] the people who come to you are the very people you need in relation to your commitment ... You are not acting individually any longer, but out of the unfolding generative order. This is the unbroken

wholeness of the implicate order out of which seemingly discrete events take place. At this point your life becomes a series of predictable miracles.[62]

Jaworski's prescription parallels a very differently-derived view, that of the psychoanalyst Bion. To make findings about others, says Bion, we must impose on ourselves 'a positive discipline of eschewing memory and desire. I do not mean that "forgetting" is enough: what is required is a positive act of refraining from memory and desire'. He goes on: 'It may be wondered what state of mind is welcome if desires and memories are not. A term that would express approximately what I need to express is 'faith' – faith that there is an ultimate reality and truth – the unknown, unknowable, 'formless infinite'. This must be believed of every object of which the personality can be aware ...'. Bion calls such faith 'a scientific state of mind and should be recognised as such'.[63] It is only with such faith that we can make genuine findings about others.[64] It is at this point that we come into connection with the formulation by Kristeva quoted at the start of this paper: 'There is no science of the subject. Any thought mastering the subject is mystical'.

Taken together, the implication of these proposals is that whenever the kind of psychical preconditions described above are fulfilled, whether fortuitously or not, synchronicities are more likely than otherwise to occur.

Explaining the inexplicable

It will be noted that the examples of synchronicity I have tried to explain in this article are not the most extreme. This raises the question: how might one explain such extreme cases of clairvoyance as that of a woman in England who had a nightmare that a mother and three children, all strangers, were trying to flee a freak fire on a liner near Paraguay and awoke to find that her dream was true? Or of the man who was forced to leave a meeting, suddenly filled with dread for his parents, and found hours later that they had died in a car accident at just the time he was overcome?

In my view, just one further proposal would need to be added to those argued in this paper to explain this extreme category of synchronicity. And this underlines the power of my approach. The proposal is, that there is some basis for a real co-ordination between the psychical and the physical dimensions of the cosmos. Thus, the semantic connectedness in the synchronic between the observably present and related but absent events would, in at least some cases, have a material dimension such that, when the car accident occurred and the man's parents died, the world would not only objectively be changed, but simultaneously, it would subjectively change the synchronic field which constituted his reality. The idea that the physical and the mental are one and the same is of course fundamental to philosophical monism as well as many contemporary approaches to brain science.[65] Thus this proposition is not new or controversial in itself. What is new is that the 'material mind' is not individualised but collective. Once again, this is not new or controversial, as widely-held theories assuming inter-subjectivity and inter-mentality show.[66]

Put the two propositions together, however, and at once we enter a domain most often trodden by the theorists of modern physics, attempting to succeed where Einstein failed – by producing a 'unified field' theory. See, for example, Capra or Davies on 'superforce,' Bohm's theory of 'implicate order' and Sheldrake's impressive accumulation of evidence for 'formative causation' leading to a universal 'morphic resonance'.[67] Whatever the eventual fate of these theories, the very fact of the convergence of the psychological arguments mounted here with the cosmic preoccupations of modern physics shows at least one or two things, depending on your viewpoint. Discursively, it shows the unifying power of cultural mythology in intellectual life.[68] Epistemologically, it suggests that the touchstone for the scientific nature of critical psychology may better be looked for 'later,' in the emergent properties of a mature, free-standing and autochthonous discipline, than as being something 'fundamental' that must be either adopted or disowned 'at the start' of one's training, depending on whether or not one is prepared to play the role of the value-cleansed experimentalist.[69]

The convergence of the discourses of physics with psychology may be expected to throw up more and more in their areas of overlap that pertains to synchronicity. For example, while from a diachronic causal approach to explanation, acts of pre-cognition (knowing about something before it happens) are inexplicable, the approach from synchrony puts events in the present, the past and the future on an equal footing in the ravelling-up of sense that produces human subjectivity.

Pragmatism, for instance, makes what 'later' becomes of an event the ultimate test of its meaning.[70] Meanwhile, on 7 August 2000, we heard that American physicists have discovered a weightless pulse that exceeds the speed of light, 'leaving the accelerator before it enters,' and hence reversing temporal ordering in just the way that a causally-oriented Victorian physics finds inconceivable.

Summary and conclusions

This paper makes sense of synchronicity by viewing it from within the purview of Saussure's concept of synchrony. The idea that there is, in Jung's words, an a-causal connecting principle that links coincident events echoes almost directly Saussure's idea that psychological events primarily make sense due to their relationships to the set of concurrent events from which they are differentiated. What is distinctive about the kinds of synchronicity that I illustrate near the start of this paper is that the pairs of events which seem anomalous are not different from each other but very similar or the same. I conclude that contemporary psychology is particularly ill-equipped to deal with synchronicitous events because it largely eschews the synchronic analysis of psychological phenomena, preferring to construe the psyche diachronically.

I suggest that, once one has recognised the salience of the synchronic in psychology, and in particular the kinds of phenomena that have led psychologists to argue the need for a concept of intersubjectivity in the analysis of infant, adult, experimental and animal behaviour, synchronicity becomes less inexplicable.[71] Indeed, I argue that, from a macro-social perspective, synchronicity is quite banal. Any enduring society must partly consist in apparatuses for reproducing both the material and subjective conditions for its own perpetuation. Hence human beings repeatedly find themselves in circumstances where others are potentially constituted in much the same way as themselves. I propose that these processes of social and material synchronisation may be complemented by processes of psychical synchronisation, potentially leading to a co-ordination of different individuals' experience. I argue that these processes of psychical co-ordination must have two aspects, an organisational aspect which permits the creation of something approaching an ideal speech-situation, and a subjective, agentive stance amongst participants of negative capability. In a brief review, I suggest that it is at this point that a wide variety of different formulations of such a stance become relevant to the discussion of synchronicity. These formulations range from the poetic, through the pragmatic and psychoanalytic, to the spiritual.

I would like to conclude by briefly addressing the question: how is synchronicity relevant to the project of critical psychology? I make three points. First, I have wanted to show that, as suggested by deconstructive principles, to focus on a topic that has largely been excluded from previous discussions in academic psychology is to reveal limitations of the discipline that go far beyond the particular topic considered. In this case, I argue that the eclipse of synchronicity is symptomatic of a more general failure to recognise the indispensability of synchronic analysis to psychology. Second, I have aimed to show that a phenomenon that is quite familiar to everyday experience need not be derided as an old wives' tale or an archaic relic of pre-scientific superstition. By adding some quite prosaic points from texts central to the critical movement in psychology[72] to some fairly uncontroversial observations from the study of experimental artefacts and intersubjectivity, one soon develops a framework within which such phenomena as telepathy or clairvoyance do not seem inimical to explanation.

This should not be surprising, for telepathy and other forms of synchronicity are generally seen as challenges to psychological individualism.[73] Likewise critical psychologists have sought to emphasise the supra-individual way in which subjectivity is produced: by individuals' incorporation into discursive practices.[74] Hence critical psychology has already elaborated a way of viewing subjectivity as something synchronised by means of processes that both transcend and are invisible to individual subjects – in just the way that commentators on synchronicity propose.

Lastly, I would like to return to the implication of Althusser's commentary on Lenin's analysis of the Russian revolution. As mentioned above, Lenin described a revolutionary time as being a time when all ideological and material contradictions coincide. This suggests that one way of furthering social liberation is for critical psychologists to develop and exploit methods which serve to synchronise, then explicate, social and psychical contradictions.[75] Such is the rationale explicitly developed for the techniques described in Freire's 'pedagogy of the oppressed' and Boal's 'theatre of the oppressed'.[76] I conclude, therefore, that were critical psychologists to develop and promote processes of psychical synchronisation, these would, once their fruit have been collectively reflected upon, prove a significant fulcrum for overturning psychological and social oppression.

Notes

A version of this paper was delivered in a symposium on 'Spirituality and Embodiment' at the Millennium Conference of Critical Psychology, University of Western Sydney, 30.04.1999. I thank the many people who have talked to me about their synchronicitous experiences over the years, the convenors of the Millennium Conference for providing a venue where these ideas did not seem too out of place, and Jane Selby, Amanda Middleton, Simone Silberberg, Merv Bendle, Emma McCormack and Mike Shelley for comments on various drafts of this paper.

1. J. Kristeva, *Revolution in Poetic Language*, Columbia University, New York 1974/1984, p215.
2. K.J. Gergen, *Invitation to Social Construction*, Sage, London 1999, p47. Note a signal quirk of the discipline's vocabulary here. If psychology is defined as the study (-ology) of the psyche, one would expect the adjective for the discipline's phenomena would be psychic or psychical. Yet if we talk of psychical phenomena in psychology, people think we are referring to such things as telepathy or clairvoyance. So, in order to distance them from any such imputation perhaps, psychologists generally refer to such topics as memory or thought as *psychological* phenomena (i.e. pertaining to psychology). Yet when a boy says he is thinking, he is not doing something psychological. He may well know nothing about the academic discipline of psychology. He is doing something with his mind or psyche; his thinking is *psychical*. Consistent with the argument advanced in this paper, I will revert to the use of the words 'psychic' and 'psychical' to mean 'pertaining to the psyche.' I will use the word 'psychological' to refer to the discipline of psychology.
3. A.J. Giddens, *The Constitution of Society: Outline of the Theory of Structuration*, Polity Press, Cambridge 1984.
4. See for example V. Walkerdine, 'From Context to Text: A Psycho-Semiotic Approach to Abstract Thought', in M. Beveridge (ed), *Children Thinking Through Language*, Arnold, London 1982.
5. See for example B. Johnson, *A World of Difference*, Johns Hopkins University Press, Baltimore 1989.
6. Cf. R. J. Hetherington, 'Sacred Cows and White Elephants', *Bulletin of the British Psychological Society*, 36, 1983, pp273-280.
7. E. E. Evans-Pritchard, *Witchcraft, Oracles and Magic among the Azande* (abridged edition), Clarendon Press, Oxford 1937/1976, p11.

8. C. G. Jung, *Synchronicity: An Acausal Connecting Principle*, Princeton University Press, Princeton 1952/1973, ppxxiv-xxv.

9. H.J. Eysenck & D.K.B Nias, *Astrology: Science or Superstition?*, Temple Smith, London 1982.

10. W. James, 'Reflections of a Psychical Researcher', in *Essays on Psychical Research*, Harvard University Press, Cambridge, Ma. 1909/1975.

11. S. Freud, 'Psychoanalysis and Telepathy', in G. Devereux (ed), *Psychoanalysis and the Occult*, International Universities Press, New York 1921 and 1922/1953; F. Hann-Kende, 'On the Role of Transference and Countertransference in Psychoanalysis', in G. Devereux (ed), *Psychoanalysis and the Occult*, International Universities Press, New York 1933/1953; H. Deutsch, 'Occult Processes Occurring During Psychoanalysis', in G. Devereux (ed), *Psychoanalysis and the Occult*, International Universities Press, New York 1926/1953.

12. See D. J. Bem & C. Honorton, 'Does Psi Exist? Replicable Evidence for an Anomalous Process of Information Transfer', *Psychological Bulletin*, 115, 1994, pp4-18.

13. M.J. Schlitz & S. LaBerge, 'Covert Observation Increases Skin Conductance in Subjects Unaware of When They are Being Observed: A Replication', *Journal of Parapsychology*, 61, 1997, pp185-196.

14. C. G. Jung, *op. cit.*, p25.

15. F. de Saussure, *Course in General Linguistics*, Penguin Books, Harmondsworth 1917/1974, p18

16. *Ibid.*, p80.

17. *Ibid.*, p89.

18. E. E. Evans-Pritchard, *op. cit.*

19. C. G. Jung, *op. cit.*, p69.

20. Viz. the 'genetic fallacy': W. James, 'Remarks on Spencer's Definition of Mind as Correspondence', in *Essays in Philosophy*, Harvard University Press, Cambridge, MA 1878/1978; W. James, *The Varieties of Religious Experience*, Penguin Books, Harmondsworth 1903/1982, Ch.1; T. Z. Lavine, 'Some reflections on the Genetic Fallacy', *Social Research*, 29, 1962, pp321-336; J. Hillman & M. Ventura, 'The revolutionary cell', in *We've Had a Hundred Years of Psychotherapy and the World's Getting Worse*, Harper Collins, New York 1992; B. S. Bradley, 'The question of Genesis', forthcoming, Manuscript to be submitted, School of Social Sciences and Liberal Studies, Charles Sturt University, Bathurst, NSW, 2795.

21. C. G. Jung *op. cit.*

22. A. Lemaire, *Jacques Lacan*, Routledge & Kegan Paul, London 1977.

23. F. de Saussure, *op. cit.*, p123.

24. W. James, *The Principles of Psychology*, Harvard University Press, Cambridge, Ma. 1890/1981, p573.

25. Cf. J. Derrida, 'Freud and the Scene of Writing', in P. Meisel (ed), *Freud: A Collection of Critical Essays*, Prentice-Hall, Englewood Cliffs, NJ 1981.

26. H.H. Bulthoff & A.L. Yuille, 'Bayesian Models for Seeing Shapes and

Depth', *Theoretical Biology*, 2, 1991, p286.

27. F. de Saussure, *op. cit.*, p120.
28. Cf. E. M. Forster, *The Machine Stops and Other Stories*, Andre Deutsch, London 1997.
29. L. Althusser, 'Ideology and Ideological State Apparatuses: Notes Towards an Investigation', in B. R. Cosin (ed), *Education: Structure and Society*, Penguin Books, Harmondsworth 1971/1972, p243.
30. *Ibid.*, p270.
31. *Ibid.*, p278.
32. L. Althusser, *For Marx*, New Left Books, London 1977.
33. V. Walkerdine, *op. cit.*, p129.
34. J. M Selby, 'Feminine Identity and Contradiction: Women Research Students at 1984', Cambridge University, PhD Thesis, Darwin College, Cambridge University; J. Henriques, W. Hollway, C. Urwin, C. Venn & V. Walkerdine, *Changing the Subject: Psychology, Social Regulation and Subjectivity*, Routledge, London (second edition) 1998.
35. See, for example, C.B. Trevarthen, 'The Self Born in Intersubjectivity: The Psychology of an Infant Communicating', in U. Neisser (ed), *The Perceived Self: Ecological and Interpersonal Sources of Self-Knowledge*, Cambridge University Press, Cambridge 1993; cf. W.S. Condon & L.W. Sander, 'Neonate Movement is Synchronised with Adult Speech: Interactional Participation and Language Acquisition', *Science*, 183, 1974, pp99-101; J.S. Watson, 'Perception of Contingency as a Determinant of Social Responsiveness', in E.B. Thoman (ed), *Origins of the Infant's Social Responsiveness*, Wiley, New Jersey 1977; R. Rosenthal & K.L. Fode, 'The Effects of Experimenter Bias on the Performance of the Albino Rat', *Behavioural Science*, 8, 1963 pp183-190; D. McIlwain, 'Consciousness: Epiphenomenon or Therapeutic Essential', paper delivered to the Biennial Conference of the International Society for Theoretical Psychology, Sydney, Australia 1999.
36. W. R. Bion, *Experiences in Groups*. Tavistock, London 1961.
37. E.g., splitting, denial; cf. M. Klein, 'Notes on Some Schizoid Mechanisms', in *Envy and Gratitude and Other Essays*, Hogarth, London 1946/1973.
38. J. Condry & S. Condry, 'Sex Differences; A Study of the Eye of the Beholder', *Child Development*, 47, 1976, pp812-819; J.Z. Rubin, F.J. Provenzano & Z. Luria, 'The Eye of the Beholder: Parents' Views on Sex of Newborns', *American Journal of Orthopsychiatry*, 44, 1974, pp512-519.
39. B. Sylvester-Bradley & C.B. Trevarthen, 'Babytalk as An Adaptation to the Infant's Communication', in N. Waterson & C. Snow (eds), *The Development of Communication*, Wiley, London 1978; C. Paul & F. Salo-Thomson, 'Infant-led Innovations in a Mother-Baby Therapy Group', *Journal of Child Psychotherapy*, 23, 1997, pp219-244.
40. J. Zinner & R. Shapiro, 'Projective Identification as a Mode of Perception and Behaviour in Families of Adolescents', *International Journal of Psychoanalysis*, 53, 1972, pp523-530.

41. J. Strouse, *Alice James: A Biography*, Houghton Mifflin, Boston 1981, pp.99-100 & 123-4.

42. S. Hall & T. Jefferson (eds), *Resistance Through Rituals: Youth Subcultures in Postwar Britain*, Routledge, London 1993.

43. Research by L. M. Murray & C. B. Trevarthen, 'Emotional Regulation of Interactions Between Two-month-olds and Their Mothers', in T.M. Field & N.A. Fox (eds), *Social Perception in Infants*, Ablex, Norwood, NJ 1985, and E. Z. Tronick, 'Emotions and Emotional Communication in Infants, *American Psychologist*, 44, 1989, pp112-119, on the experimental perturbation of infant-mother interactions shows how much babies dislike being out of sync with their mothers.

44. V. Walkerdine, *op. cit.*

45. D. Bohm, *Wholeness and the Implicate Order*, Routledge & Kegan Paul, London 1980.

46. D. McIlwain, *op. cit.*; N. Stephenson, 'Being Clichéd: Women's Talk and Feminine Subjectivities', Paper delivered at the Biennial Conference of the International Society for Theoretical Psychology, Sydney, Australia, April, 1999.

47. Cf. W. James, 'Does "Consciousness" Exist?', in *Essays in Radical Empiricism*, Longman's, New York 1904/1912; N. Rose, *Inventing Our Selves: Psychology, Power and Personhood*, Cambridge University Press, Cambridge 1996.

48. P. Freire, *Pedagogy of the Oppressed*, Penguin Books, Harmondsworth 1970; B.S. Bradley, (2000). 'The Role of Values in Psychology: Implications for a Reformed Curriculum', in M. Leicester & C. Modgil (eds), *Values, Education and Cultural Diversity*, Falmer Press, London 2000.

49. J. Lacan, *The Four Fundamental Concepts of Psychoanalysis*, Penguin Books, Harmondsworth 1977.

50. W. Bion, *op. cit.*, 1961.

51. J. Habermas, 'Toward a Theory of Communicative Competence', in H.P. Dreitzel (ed), *Recent Sociology No.2*, Macmillan, London 1970.

52. A. Giddens, *op. cit.*

53. B. Davies, *Post-Structuralist Theory and Classroom Practice*, Deakin University Press, Geelong, Victoria 1994.

54. A. Boal, *Games for Actors and Non-Actors*, Routledge, London 1992.

55. J. Keats, Letter to George and Tom Keats (21 or 27 December 1817), in R. Gittings (ed), *Letters of John Keats*, Oxford University Press, Oxford 1817/1970.

56. V. N. Voloshinov, *Marxism and the Philosophy of Language*, Seminar Press, New York 1973; cf. 'inner voice' in J. Jaworski, *Synchronicity: The Inner Path of Leadership*, Berrett-Koehler, San Francisco 1996.

57. M. Milner, *The Suppressed Madness of Sane Men: Forty-Four Years of Exploring Psychoanalysis*, Routledge, London 1988; J.M. Selby, 'Uncertainty in Couselling and Psychotherapy', in *Proceedings of the Third National*

Conference of the Alcohol and Drug Foundation, Queensland Alcohol and Drug Foundation, Brisbane 1990.

58. D.W. Winnicott, *Playing and Reality*, Penguin Books, Harmondsworth 1967; A. Game, 'The creative self', Keynote address delivered at the Biennial Conference of the International Society for Theoretical Psychology, Sydney, Australia, 27 April 1999.

59. G. Devereux, *From Anxiety to Method in the Behavioural Sciences*, Mouton, The Hague 1967; J. M. Selby, 'Cross-Cultural Research in Health Psychology: Illustrations from Australia', in K. Chamberlain & M. Murray (eds), *Qualitative Health Psychology*, Sage, London 1999.

60. E. Levinas, *Totality and Infinity: An Essay on Interiority*, Duquesne University Press, Pittsburgh 1969; B.S. Bradley & J.M. Selby, 'Therapy, Consciousness-Raising and Revolution', in I. Parker & R. Spears (eds), *Psychology and Society: Radical Theory and Practice*, Pluto Press, London 1996.

61. G. Ross, *Is There Life Before Death? Reflections on our Spiritual Awakening*, ABC Books, Sydney 1999, p151.

62. J. Jaworski, *op. cit.*, pp184-5.

63. W.R. Bion, *Attention and Interpretation: A Scientific Approach to Insight in Psycho-Analysis and Groups*, Tavistock, London 1970, pp31-32.

64. Cf. S. Weil, *Gravity and Grace*, Routledge & Kegan Paul, London 1963.

65. For example, of Spinoza, or D. Davidson, 'The Material Mind', in *Essays on Actions and Events*, Clarendon, Oxford 1980.

66. See, for example, W. Bion, *op. cit.*, 1961; L. Vygotsky, *Mind in Society: the Development of Higher Psychological Processes*, Harvard University Press, Cambridge, Ma. 1978; Trevarthen, *op. cit.*

67. F. Capra, *The Tao of Physics*, Wildwood, London 1974; P.C. W. Davies, *Superforce*, Heinemann, London 1984; D. Bohm, *op. cit.*; R. Sheldrake, *The Presence of the Past: Morphic Resonance and the Habits of Nature*, Park Street Press, Rochester, VT 1995.

68. Cf. R. Barthes, *Mythologies*, Paladin, London 1956/1973.

69. Cf. I.D. John, '"The Scientist" as Role Model for "The Psychologist"', *Australian Psychologist*, 21, 1986, pp219-240.

70. B.S. Bradley, *op. cit.*, 1998.

71. Cf. J. Habermas, *op. cit.*; C.B. Trevarthen, *op. cit.*; D.N. Stern, *The Interpersonal World of the Infant: A View from Psychoanalysis and Developmental Psychology*, Basic Books, New York 1985; J.M. Suls & R.L. Rosnow, 'Concerns About Artifacts in Psychological Experiments', in J.G. Morawski (ed), *The Rise of Experimentation in American Psychology*, Yale University Press, New Haven 1988.

72. F. de Saussure, L. Althusser; cf. Henriques et al., *op. cit.*

73. For example D.J. Bem & C. Honorton, *op. cit.*; M.J. Schlitz & S. LaBerge, *op. cit.*

74. C. Urwin, 'Power Relations and the Emergence of Language', in J. Henriques, W. Hollway, C. Urwin, C. Venn & V. Walkerdine, *Changing the*

Subject: Psychology, Social Regulation and Subjectivity, op. cit.

75. B.S. Bradley & J. R Morss, 'Social Construction in a World at Risk: 'Towards a Psychology of Experience', *Theory & Psychology*, (under review).

76. A. Boal, *op. cit.*

Participatory action research behind bars

Michelle Fine, Rosemarie A. Roberts, María Elena Torre and Debora Upegui

Within the global, mass criminalisation of poor and working class men and women, we have carved a space for a participatory research project conducted by six women inside a maximum security correctional facility and four women at City University of New York, (CUNY) Graduate Center. Our collaborative research project is designed to interrogate the consequences of college on women in prison, the prison environment, the women's children and the women's post-release outcomes. Moreover, we work with a community-based organising project designed toward broad-based public education about the proliferation and consequences of mass imprisonment, particularly within communities of colour. This piece of scholarship walks a political and intellectual tightrope, only part of which can be elaborated in text. As we author and co-author multiple essays for very different audiences, this piece was requested by Valerie Walkerdine a bit 'early' in our agreements for State review and therefore full team-authorship. Thus we write, this time as the CUNY half of the team, with profound respect for the women inside and worries about the vulnerabilities of speaking without approval.

We write this memo, as a work in progress, to educate and outrage, and to raise evidence and questions about the politics, theorising, ethics and methods of participatory research. We write, together, under and against surveillance, hoping to create a fissure in the global and increasingly-privatised practices of massive imprisonment. We write this text in two 'registers': first, to simply reveal the breadth of the problem, with an analysis of race, class and gender, and then, to introduce the power and complexities of participatory research behind bars. Like many before us, we sought to organise all aspects of the intervention and the research through democratic participation. And like those before, our practice did not always live up to the design. In the spirit of Brinton Lykes, Linda Tuhiwai Smith and Ignacio Martín-Baró,[1] we recognise profoundly the relative freedom and therefore responsibility of outside researchers to speak critically and constructively about the possibilities and limits of participatory education within the walls of prison.

Surrounded by a resounding and global discourse of disposability, young men and women throughout the United States, and around the globe, are being exiled in their own nations beyond the lines of citizenship, into spaces for the banished, stripped of rights, deemed unworthy, unredeemable, and a burden to the 'booming economies' and 'unprecedented' financial growth. Indeed, across the United States and the countries of so many readers, we witness the dismantling of the public sphere, twinned with a discourse of disposability tattooed onto the souls of youth and adults who are poor and working class, typically African American and Latino, always dispossessed. They may be native, indigenous, or immigrant at the bottom of a caste or class system. They have witnessed a discursive brutality about what 'they' are taking from 'us', matched only by the material devastation that brands them, and their children, as they no longer belonging on 'our' streets, in 'our' schools, restaurants, neighbourhoods, on 'our' welfare rolls (now reserved for multinational corporations) and certainly not in 'our' universities or workplaces. It would be inaccurate to argue that the State has simply walked away from poor and working class men and women, particularly men and women of colour. What they are getting instead, here and globally, on the State's bill, are prisons.

The differential incarceration rates by race, ethnicity and class are dramatic. African Americans, who comprise 13 per cent of the US population, constitute a full half of the 1.2 million state and federal prisoners.[2] With Latinos, people of colour in the United States account for two thirds of all state and federal prisoners.[3] In 1995, one of every three African American men between 20 and 29 was in prison, jail, on parole or probation; a full 13 per cent of African American adult males have lost the right to vote, with some states reaching up to 40 per cent.[4] By gender and race, incarceration rates for women are rising faster than any other category of prisoners nation-wide, an increase of 573 per cent from 1980 to 1997, compared to an increase of 294 per cent for males during the same period.[5]

Between 1986 and 1996, the number of women incarcerated in state prisons for drug offence rose by 888 per cent in contrast to 129 per cent for non-drug offenses.[6] In New York State, drug offences account for 91 per cent of the increase in women's incarceration between 1986 and 1995, a direct result of enforcement of the Rockefeller Drug Laws, which mandate sentences of fifteen years to life for any person selling two ounces or possessing four ounces of an illegal substance. A full 91 per cent of prison sentences for drugs are meted out to African American and Latino women, who comprise 32 per cent of the state population.[7] Though these statistics appear to suggest a new wave in women's criminal activity, in reality, they reflect a dramatic shift in the policies of the prison-industrial complex.

Public support for higher education for men and women in prison

From the mid 1970s through 1995, Federal Pell grants, matched with State based TAP dollars, enabled men and women in prison to enrol in college courses and, in some instances, earn an associate's, bachelor's or even master's degree. In 1994, President Clinton signed the Violent Crime Control and Law Enforcement Act, which meant that convicted felons were no longer eligible for Pell grants. (Only one tenth of 1 per cent of Pell grants were awarded to persons in prisons or jails). With public funds for college education in prisons eliminated, the existent college programme at the site of our work, sponsored by a local College for fifteen years, closed, as did over three hundred other college programmes sponsored in prisons nation-wide.

Within months of these cuts, a Task Force of community representatives from the county, local college presidents, a group of inmates and the prison administration strategised to bring college back to the facility. In an incredible instance of community organising and grass-roots activism, in the fall of 1997 a BA in sociology programme was launched. At the heart of the new college design were fundamental principles of democratic practice:

- a commitment to critical intellectual growth for individual students;
- a pre-college programme to prepare the majority of students who were not yet high school/GED graduates;
- structures to insure a strong, inmate-based community of learners, tutors and mentors among the women in the college, and
- deep inmate participation in the design, ongoing evaluation and running of the college programme.

On the ground, these principles meant that students were expected to be engaged in rigorous academic work. As well, a committee of prison administrators, educators and inmates generated guidelines for inmate participation, responsibility and giving back. All women pay a fee of $10 per semester (the approximate equivalent of a month's wages), for their education. Inmates and outside volunteers agreed that such payment would be politically and psychologically significant during times when poor and working class people not in prison are indeed having a hard time affording higher education (and deeply resentful of 'freebies' to inmates). Classes are offered in the evening, after a day of work. Additionally, women commit to hours of service within the facility and they promise to tutor other women while in the facility.

At the moment of writing this, June 2000, close to three hundred women have participated in the college programme, with many more involved in the pre-college programme. Fewer than half of the women in the facility come with a twelfth-grade education or an equivalency degree; more than 75 per cent carry histories of drug and/or alcohol abuse; 80 per cent self-report histories of child and/or adult sexual, physical or emotional abuse; about half are on the rolls of the Mental Health division, with more than half of these on medication. The average sentence for a woman at this facility is 8 1/3 years, with two hundred of the six hundred women in the active population serving far more than that. Fifty percent are African American, 28 per cent Latina, 19 per cent Caucasian and 5 per cent Asian; a fair number are immigrants. We offer these statistics not to heighten the moral panic and spectacularising around the women, but to note that these are the women who have paid a heavy price for global capitalism, the right wing assault on the public sector, vicious racism and the punishing of girls and women in homes, on the streets, by the State and the economy.

It is in this context, with these women of 'vision and dignity, style and persistence,' as a recent graduate described them, that we under-took a participatory research project on the impact of college. We see the research as both an analysis of college as a transformative practice within a 'para-military' organisation (self description of the organisa-tion); and we see the research as a vehicle for organising around broader issues of mass incarceration of poor and working class youth and young adults of colour.

> In the participatory research propounded here, the silenced are not just incidental to the curiosity of the researcher but are the masters of inquiry into the underlying causes of the events in their world.[8]

To begin the participatory work, we read together and separately the works of participatory action researchers to invent a practice that was fundamentally feminist and critical, that could be deployed under, and against, surveillance. We drew from: Kurt Lewin, who, in the 1940s, dared to assert participant knowledge as foundational to valid-ity, democratic and participatory research as foundational to social change.

Central and South American theorists and practitioners, including Orlando Fals-Borda, Paulo Freire and Ignacio Martín-Baró, have, more recently, extended the commitments to participatory action research (PAR) well beyond the borders of psychology, into an explicit analysis of the relation of science to social inequality, community life and radi-cal social change, rejecting 'the terms of reference (and) the categories operating within the standard sociological paradigms imported from Europe and the United States [as] ideologically corrupted in defending the interests of the "dominant bourgeoisie"'.[9] With similar commit-ments, Hans Toch authored a powerful article, in 1967, which spoke about PAR in prison, explicating a set of design-principles which endorse relying upon 'convicts' as co-researchers.[10]

In the last five years, with a feminist, critical and explicitly anti-colonial turn, the writings on the stance of participatory researchers have broken important new ground. Our work has been enormously influenced by five such turns. To begin, there has been a sharp recog-nition of participation *with*, not only *for*, oppressed peoples. Psychologist Brinton Lykes marks this move in her language, reflect-ing her stance on a project in which she "agreed to *accompany* a friend to her community of origin in the Highlands of Guatemala ... [recognising myself] as a 'situated other' within a *praxis of solidarity* [which] informs my ongoing efforts to develop alternative methods for 'standing under' these realities and participating with local actors in responding to problems in daily living".[11]

Second, we read and drew from standpoint theorists and critical race and legal theorists, who demand a recognition of the intellectual power and searing social commentary developed at the bottom of social formations.[12] Third, from the growing literature on research for and by indigenous peoples, we have drawn from the writings of Maori theorist and researcher Linda Tuhiwai Smith, who recognises not only the powerful wisdom accumulated in indigenous communities but also that indigenous values, beliefs and behaviours must be incorporated and theorised into the praxis of participatory research.[13]

Fourth, the writings of critical psychologist Kum Kum Bhavnani have encouraged us to struggle aloud with questions of objectivity within self-consciously political research.[14] Bhavnani asks scholars to write toward: *inscription*, producing social analyses which challenge dominant scripts; the *micro-politics of research*, whereby researchers explicitly analyse our relations to and with the 'subjects' of our research; and *difference*, which requires that researchers seek to understand the subtle and significant 'differences' within any category of social analysis.

Fifth, we take seriously the writings of Glenda Russell and J. Bohan, who argue that it is crucial to theorise and strategize how PAR 'gives back' to communities good enough to open themselves up for intellectual scrutiny.[15]

We create among us: A team of women scholars

Among us, as a team, we meet often, sometimes once a month, sometimes more or less, always profoundly encumbered by limitations on privacy, freedom, contact and time, and always as profoundly moved by our shared capacity and desire to climb over the walls that separate us we carve a small delicate space of trust, reciprocity and the ability to argue respectfully about what was important to study, to speak, and to hold quietly among ourselves.

We seek to create a small community of women who invented the possibility of shared commitments to co operation, mutuality and support [and to critical inquiry] ... A 're-viewing' to involve us in the continuing constitution and renewal of a common world, if we [could] keep in mind the idea that such a world may come into being in the course of a continuing dialogue, which we ourselves can provoke and nurture in the midst of change ... using [our] imaginations, taping [our] courage – "to transform"'.[16]

In this space for critical inquiry, among us, we walk across barbed wires outside the windows and inside the room, through our racialised and classed histories, between biographies filled with too much violence and too little hope, and biographies lined with too much privilege and too little critique. We speak in whispers and codes as officers walk by, and laugh too loudly, as though we were truly in a safe space. We engaged in what Paulo Freire would call 'dialogue'. In contrast to what he called 'magic consciousness characterised by fatalism, which leads men (sic) to fold their arms, resigned to the impossibility of resisting the power of facts',[17] Freire (and so, we too) sought to create educational spaces, in which 'facts' were submitted to analysis, 'causes' reconsidered, and structural and personal 'responsibility' reconceived in biographic and historical context.

Between us: positioned inside and out

We are, at once, a team of semi-fictional coherence, and, on the ground, a group of women living very different lives, defined in part by biographies of class, race and ethnic differences. Half of us go home at night; half of us live in prison. Many of us bring personal histories of violence against women to our work, while all of us worry about violence against, and sometimes by, women. Some of us have long-standing experience in social movements for social justice; others barely survived on the outside. Some of us are white, Jewish, Latina, Caribbean, African American, some 'mixed'. Most of us are from the mainland of this country, a few born outside the borders of the US. The most obvious 'divide' among us is free or imprisoned, but the other tattoos and scars on our souls weave through our work, worries, writings and our many communities. Usually these differences enrich us. Sometimes they distinguish us. At moments they separate us. We understand ourselves to carry knowledge and consciousness that are, at once, determined by where we come from, and shaped by who we choose to be.[18] As bell hooks has written, 'This space of radical openness is a margin – a profound edge. Locating oneself there is difficult yet necessary. It is not a "safe" place. One is always at risk. One needs a community of "resistance"'.[19]

Among us, a woman inside writes that, 'Most research on prisons is conducted by outside investigators. However, there is an incredible source of skills right inside these walls. Convict researchers can establish a comfort-zone with interviewees that many outside researchers cannot. Because a lot of people in prison are less trusting of outsiders, they may not be entirely forthcoming with their responses. However, inmate researchers, by the nature of their status as inmates, are often viewed by participants as more trustworthy. ... Just because I am in prison does not negate the fact that I am also a competent researcher. Using prisoners as researchers is a valuable experience that is beneficial to both the subjects of the study and the readers of the "results"'.

Together we have designed a project that has six streams of data collection: inmate initiated research projects, in which each of thirteen women interviewed at least five others on questions of her own signature (e.g., How does college affect spiritual life? What are the particular issues of college for women who have experienced violence since childhood and into adulthood? What are the effects of college on the children of students? What are the differential experiences for women from different social classes and academic histories? We then co-facilitated focus groups, one inside and one outside researcher, with seven groups, comprised of women who did not finish college; women in the Adult Basic Education and GED programmes, women who initiated the college programme, first-time college students, women whose primary language is not English; the teen children of women in college, and graduates. Third, we have conducted life histories with fifteen women who graduated from college and are no longer in prison. Fourth, the State is conducting a recidivism study for us, tracking the re-imprisonment rates of college going vs. non-college going women who have been in prison. Fifth, we are in the midst of interviewing correctional officers. And sixth, we have surveyed the full faculty (thirty participants) about their views on and experiences within the college programme.

In other words, we sit, sleep and dream surrounded by the words, wisdom, worries and contradictions of women once, now or forever living behind bars.

Speedbumps: spots in our work where we stop to consider questions that linger, responsibilities that can't be fulfilled, vulnerabilities, and critical legacies within and beyond the prison.

A number of feminist and critical race theorists join participatory researchers to reveal what Venezuelan community psychologist Esther Weisenfeld has called the 'unfulfilled promises of PAR'.[20] Patricia Maguire writes on her training of participatory researchers in the new South Africa and reports a low-level but pervasive resistance to the dialogic, non-authoritarian nature of the work.[21] Anne Bettencourt notes with concern that, once a compelling project is stirred up, participatory researchers often fail to relinquish control to the interior leadership structure.[22] Cynthia Chataway offers a very careful analysis of her work with a Native American community, respectfully recognising that those who live in communities that are oppressed and under surveillance may, indeed, insist upon privacy – non-publication of results – as a form of public responsibility.[23] Likewise, Linda Tuhiwai Smith reminds us that indigenous people have well-earned fears about the further loss of their intellectual and cultural knowledges and may, therefore, resist even the most participatory of researchers.[24]

We hear all of these cautions as wisdom. We too have learned, as Linda Tuhiwai Smith would warn us, that what appears to be paranoia may just be hard-earned local wisdom and not to confuse 'finding your voice' or 'speaking out' with courage – not in a maximum security prison – even one of the best. We have learned that 'equal' participation and responsibility do not mean the 'same' but, instead, endless ongoing conversations among us, with every decision always re-visited about who can take risks, who dares to speak, who must remain quiet and what topics need never see the light of day. As Linda Martín Alcoff has written, we are painfully aware that we always need to 'analyse the probable or actual effects of [our] words on the [many, contradictory] discursive and material contexts "[both within and beyond the walls of prison.]"'.[25]

Issues of epistemology, theory, methods, ethics, writing and interpretation keep us up at night. Below we give you a preview of our top eight collective headaches to date:

- *Resisting Surveillance.* How do we design our work so as not to heighten the surveillance on women who have already paid too high a price for global capitalism and racism?

- *Theorising and Interrupting Representations of Pathology.* How do we theorise and interrupt the layers of discursive pathologising of inmates – inmates of colour, women inmates, mothers who kill – writing against these representations as we recognise that they flood the audiences of our work?

- *Exploiting and Troubling notions of expertise and experience.* What role do 'expertise' and 'experience' play (productively and perversely) in policy conversations and in community organising? To what extent do we trade on race and class privilege toward a project of social justice; that is, gaining an audience of influence? Can we lend ourselves to 'channel' these voices, agitating for social justice in arenas from which these women are barred?

- *Vulnerability.* How do we minimise the vulnerability of women inside and still speak critically about the transformative power of education and devastating, racist consequences of mass incarceration?

- *Critical Consciousness – for whom? To what end?* If, as has been written and we have witnessed, participatory work creates a context for critical consciousness among all of us – toward what end, especially for those of us still inside and then, too, those of us outside?

- *The Psychological Discourse of Individual Blame.* It is simply the case that a discourse of individual self-blame and psychology of redemption is the path out of prison ('It was my fault; I am responsible; no social critique; "I won't do it again"'). And it is the case that the women, particularly after college, narrate both a powerful blend of social critique of class, race and, most profoundly, gendered-violence relations, and an analysis of personal mistakes made, poor judgements, individual responsibilities. Can we write, collectively, a text that walks this discursive tightrope, crediting the political without romanticising the convict, and acknowledging personal agency without colluding in the vicious ways in which she has been held accountable for the ills of global and racialised capitalism?

- *Writing to Organise and Engage a Broader Conversation.* To what extent can we use this empirical investigation into college to wedge open a larger, public conversation through the narrow needle's eye of college?

- *Audience and Ambivalence.* Can we write into and through the public's profound ambivalence – not just the presumed blood-thirsty desire for more prisons and not simply a fictionalised, broad-based hatred of prisons, but profound ambivalence – with evidence of what is, what could be and what must be available, particularly for poor and working class women to, indeed, cope with daily life on the outside –enormous violence, responsibility and very limited options?

• *Revealing the Brutality Survived by Poor Women, before and after prison.* One of the teens we interviewed told us, 'My mom never would have gotten her life together if she didn't go "to prison and then to college"'. As if in an echo, one woman told us, 'I needed to get out of my life, away from the violence, drugs, racism and poverty, to find another way. "Prison offered that to me"'. The teens and the women reveal the depths of oppression which define the everyday lives of some women living in poor, oppressed communities before and after prison. Life inside prison is no holiday. But neither is life outside. For many women, prison is the first time they are free of male violence, the pressures of sustaining families, without the temptations of drugs or the terrors of possible homelessness. College transforms much, but it doesn't dismantle capitalism, racism and sexism. We aim to write in ways that provoke a sense of possibility, within a profound structural critique.

We'll keep you posted – and next time, it will, indeed, be all of us.

Notes

1. I. Martín-Baró, *Writings for a Liberation Psychology*, Harvard University Press, Cambridge, MA 1994.
2. A. J. Beck & C. J. Mumola, *Prisoners in 1998*, Bureau of Justice Statistics, Washington, DC 1999.
3. 'The Sentencing Project', *Facts about Prisons and Prisoners*, Briefing/Fact Sheets 1035, The Sentencing Project, Washington, DC February 2000.
4. M. Mauer, *Young Black Americans in the Criminal Justice System: Five Years Later*, The Sentencing Project, Washington, DC 1995; J. Fellner & M. Mauer, *Losing the Vote: The Impact of Felony Disenfranchisement Laws in the United States*, The Sentencing Project and Human Rights Watch, Washington, DC 1998.
5. M. Mauer, C. Potler, & R. Wolf, *Gender and Justice: Women, Drugs, and Sentencing Policy*, The Sentencing Project, Washington, DC 1999.
6. *Ibid.*
7. J. Fellner & M. Mauer, *op. cit.*; M. Mauer, *op. cit.*
8. P. Freire, 'Foreword', in P. Par, M. Brydon-Miller, B. Hall, & T. Jackson

(eds), *Voices of Change: Participatory Research in the US and Canada* Bergin and Garvey, Westport, CT 1993, px.

9. O. Fals-Borda, 'Investigating the Reality in Order to Transform It', *Dialectical Anthropology*, 4, 1979, p34.

10. H. Toch, 'The Convict as Researcher', *Style and Substance in Sociology* 1967, pp497-500.

11. M.B. Lykes, 'Activist Participatory Research and the Arts with Rural Maya Women: Interculturality and Situated Meaning Making', in D.L. Tolman & M. Brydon-Miller (eds), *From Subjects to Subjectivities: A Handbook of Interpretive and Participatory Methods*, NYU Press, New York 2001, p1.

12. See, for example, b. hooks, *Feminist Theory from Margin to Center*, South End Press, Boston 1984; G. Ladson-Billings, 'Racialized Discourses and Ethnic Epistemologies', in N.K. Denzin & Y.S. Lincoln (eds), *Handbook of Qualitative Research* (2nd ed.), Sage, Thousand Oaks, CA 2000, pp257-277; M. Matsuda, 'Looking to the Bottom: Critical Legal Studies and Reparations', in K. Crenshaw, N. Gotanda, G. Peller, & K. Thomas (eds), *Critical Race Theory: The Key Writings that Formed the Movement*, New Press, New York 1996, pp63-79; A. McIntyre, *Making Meaning of Whiteness: Exploring Racial Identity with White Teachers*, SUNY Press, Albany, NY 1997; N. Piran, 'Re-inhabiting the Body from the Inside Out: Girls Transform their School Environment', in D.L. Tolman & M. Brydon-Miller (eds), *From Subjects to Subjectivities: A Handbook of Interpretive and Participatory Methods, op. cit.*

13. L.T. Smith, *Decolonizing Methodologies: Research and Indigenous Peoples*, Zed Books, London 1999.

14. K.K. Bhavnani, 'Tracing the Contours: Feminist Research and Objectivity', in H. Afshar & M. Maynard (eds), *The Dynamics of 'Race' and Gender : Some Feminist Interventions*, Taylor & Francis, London 1994, pp26-40.

15. G. Russell & J. Bohan, 'Hearing Voices: The Uses of Research and the Politics of Change', *Psychology of Women Quarterly*, 23 1999, pp403-418.

16. M. Greene, *Releasing the Imagination: Essays on Education, the Arts, and Social Change*, Jossey-Bass, San Francisco 1995, p196,198.

17. P. Freire, 'Creating Alternative Research Methods: Learning to Do it by Doing it', in B. Hall, A. Gillette, and R. Tandon (eds), *Creating Knowledge: A Monopoly*, Society for Participatory Research in Asia, New Delhi 1982, p44.

18. S. Harding, *Discovering Reality: Feminist Perspectives on Epistemology, Metaphysics, Methodology, and Philosophy of Science*, D. Reidel, Dordrecht, Holland 1983; N. C. M. Hartstock, *Money, Sex, and Power: Toward a Feminist Historical Materialism*, Longman, New York 1983; A. M. Jaggar, *Feminist Politics and Human Nature*, Rowman & Allenheld, Totowa, NJ 1983.

19. b. hooks, *Black Looks: Race and Representation*, South End Press, Boston 1992, p149.

20. E. Weisenfeld, 'The Researcher's Place in Qualitative Inquiries:

Unfulfilled Promises?' The 27th Interamerican Congress of Psychology, Caracas, Venezuela 1999; E. Weisenfeld, 'Community Social Psychology, Knowledge Construction and Participatory Action Research: What, Who and How?' Keynote in the Latin American Seminar on Community Psychology and Health, Brasilia, Brazil 1997.

21. P. Maguire, 'The Congruency Thing: Transforming Psychology—Research and Pedagogy', in D.L. Tolman & M. Brydon-Miller (eds), *From Subjects to Subjectivities: A Handbook of Interpretive and Participatory Methods, op.cit.*

22. B.A. Bettencourt, G. Dillman, & N. Wolman, 'The Intragroup Dynamics of Maintaining a Successful Grassroots Organization: A Case Study', *Journal of Social Issues*, 52 1997, pp207-220.

23. C.J. Chataway, 'An Examination of the Constraints on Mutual Inquiry in a Participatory Action Research Project', *Journal of Social Issues*, 53 1997, pp747-765.

24. L.T. Smith, *Decolonizing Methodologies: Research and Indigenous Peoples, op. cit.*

25. L.M. Alcoff, 'The Problem of Speaking for Others', in J. Roof & R. Wiegman (eds), *Who Can Speak?: Authority and Critical Identity*, University of Illinois Press, Urbana, IL 1995, p111.

Mad Pride

Russell Hall and Sybil Ahmane

The aim of Mad Pride is to gain, not only as the name suggests a sense of dignity for a condition that effects many yet still causes fear but also to plant the seeds of a movement that sees itself as the next big civil rights movement. Their use of the word 'mad' is a well known civil rights strategy of taking back a word that has, over the several hundred years been used to vilify and stigmatise people suffering mental health problems, along with 'deranged', 'lunatic', and the clinically sterile 'insane' and reclaim it. The movement also sees itself as having strong historical links with gay rights groups as Simon Barnett, a Mad Pride activist explains;

> The philosophy is that the end of the twentieth century has been dominated by civil rights movements; we've had the American civil rights movement in the 1960s, the women's movement, the gay rights movement. Perhaps we're the next one's to win our rights and some sort of freedom.[1]

The work of Foucault in particular backs up this historical connection. His work on disciplinary technologies suggests that the entry into law of medicine and psychiatry in the nineteenth century led to a process of 'normalisation' – that which is considered 'normal' as oppose to that which is considered right or wrong. Foucault believes that an essential part of the process of normalisation is the role it plays in the systematic creation, classification and control of 'anomalies' in the social body, 'anomalies' being, amongst others homosexuals and mental health sufferers. These technologies, Foucault suggests led to individuals being fixed in a web of objective codification under the auspices of medicine and the new pseudo sciences.[2]

> The madman, like the artist, is construed by us in terms of his difference from the rest of us, so construing ourselves as well as him. The outsider is perceived as a challenge to our beliefs and perceptions, like an incurable sore on the otherwise serene face of our culture.[3]

However while the gay rights movement has made steady progress over the past thirty years the user movement has, until now been less successful. A recent Mental Health Green Paper (Reform of the Mental Health Act) includes Community Treatment Orders (CTO) which put users in the community under a curfew so that medication can be given at certain times. Failure to comply with these orders will allow mental health professionals, paramedics and the Police to take the user to a place of treatment and, if necessary forcibly administer drugs.

> The planned 'mental act from hell', as it is already widely known, promises to allow the medical profession to force-feed toxic drugs to people in the community with a mental health diagnosis, in order to increase profits from pharmaceutical multinationals. 'Mad' people will continue to be incarcerated with even fewer rights of appeal than previously, and the boundaries between 'mental illness' and 'criminality' will be further blurred.[4]

The user movement itself is not a new idea; it was first talked about in the early 1970s culminating, in 1974 with the publication of what is now known as the 'Fish Pamphlet' the first manifesto written by, and for users. The originators of this document, the Mental Patients Union (MPU) evolved in the late 1970s into PROMPT (Promotion of the Rights of Mental Patients in Treatment) and finally CAPO (Campaign Against Psychiatric Oppression) in the 1980s. In recent years many more self help groups have emerged for 'survivors' of the mental health care system all campaigning for better treatment for both users, and ex-users as well as acting as 'safe' places to discuss both illness and recovery;

For many clients the group is a place where lives are shared, a place where their pain and distress is disclosed to an extent that there have been groups in which I have sat where the pain and distress is almost tangible, almost solid and very real.[5]

Also in recent years the gap between user and professional has been crossed. At a recent conference in Nottingham, the Millennium Conference, Rachael Perkins who is both a diagnosed manic-depressive and psychologist, spoke on mental health and civil rights. She pointed out that users who have been on a section at any time (involuntarily placed in hospital) are ineligible to serve on a jury, are unable to take out any form of insurance, and are restricted entry to some other countries, such as the United States. In essence this turns a medical record into a criminal record and Perkins believes that users should come together on these issues as they effect users rights to be a functioning part of society.

Other user groups are using their experiences as tools for training mental health professionals, several of whom have also worked in the system. Many users/professionals have given talks at national conferences, and many have used autobiographical accounts to offer an insight into the condition. At the recent Voices and Visions conference in Exeter 70 per cent of the attendees were service users and this illustrates the growing empowerment in the user movement.

A research study in Holland, conducted by the psychiatrist Maruis Romme, using television and radio asked people who heard voices to come forward and discuss their coping strategies. A very interesting fact was that many of these people had not been diagnosed. Romme then devised a method of treatment which involves working *with* users in order to find the meaning of the voices rather than considering them to be little more than a symptom.

Mad Pride week took place in early July 2000 and was not restricted to events in Britain. Celebrations were held in America, Canada and Africa and this clearly shows that the movement is fast becoming a world-wide phenomenon. In Britain plays which deals with the subject were performed; one of these, *Is It A Crime To Be Happy?* was written by Richard Jameson, a diagnosed manic-depressive. Other events included an overnight vigil at what is known as 'Suicide Bridge', in Archway, London during which songs were sung in memory of the users who took their lives at the bridge. For many however the main part of Mad Pride week was a one-day festival held at Clissold Park on Saturday 15 July. It was attended by approximately 1500 people and although it featured many bands, poets, speakers and information about self help groups and other user-led organisations it was primarily a chance for users to meet, discuss ideas and most importantly to be visible as an organised, issue led group. It was also a chance to take part in an event, which many feel marks a specific moment in history. The atmosphere was high spirited but peaceful, as shown by the lack of any police presence and although, interestingly there was very little media coverage of the event it is set to grow in popularity. Many users who did not, or who were unable to attend will surely be effected by the fact that the festival, organised entirely by users, has happened and next year, now that momentum is gathering there will be more events and on a larger scale.

The musical highlight of the festival for many was a set by The Larry Love Band who not only continued to play using acoustic guitars after the local council had turned off the electricity supply, but also played while the marquee was being dismantled around them. They finally took both audience and instruments to a nearby fence and played for a further forty minutes in the rapidly fading light. For many the whole event marked a watershed for 'survivors' and this final event of the day quickly took on the resonance of a peace demonstration, an unusual reversal – people coming together for a common purpose amidst the chaos of officialdom.

Mental health problems are a condition that can affect anyone regardless of class, race, age, gender or sexuality, they do not discriminate and they affect between one in six people (department of health) and one in four (Mental Health Foundation). This suggests that somewhere between ten and fifteen million people in the UK alone will, at some point in their lives be directly affected and although severe 'mental illness' is relatively uncommon, a great many people will suffer from more common conditions such as depression or anxiety. These figures suggest that as a minority group, users represent a significant percentage of the population and that Mad Pride is not only a timely reminder that in the twenty first century civil rights issues still need to be addressed but that as a movement it has the potential of being the largest civil rights group to date.

Notes

1. T. Curtis, R Dellar, E Leslie and B Watson (eds), *Mad Pride: A Celebration of Mad Culture*, Spare Change Books, London 2000, p7.
2. M. Foucault, *Discipline and Punish*, Tavistock 1977; M. Foucault, *History of Sexuality*, Penguin, Harmondsworth 1978.
3. F.A. Jenner, *Schizophrenia a Disease or Some Ways of Being Human*, Sheffield Academic Press, England 1993, p18.
4. T. Curtis et al., *op. cit.*, p7.
5. R. Coleman, *Recovery: An Alien Concept*, Handsell Publishing 1999, p71.

Ideology Criticism in Theory and Practice

Tod Sloan

At the risk of sounding totally outrageous, I will assert that the primary reason for the massive failure of academic psychology as a force for human betterment has been its inability to understand ideological processes and their role in the production of human suffering. The aim of this short commentary is to revive a critical notion of ideology and to invite psychologists to tackle the long-neglected, but crucial task of ideology criticism. This should not be necessary, for it has been done dozens of times before, but it is clear that few psychologists have grasped the import of this task.[1] For this reason, I strain throughout these comments to be as straightforward as possible.

We can begin with an example designed to illustrate the scope of the phenomena we need to comprehend as ideology: Every weekend, a billion people or so, all over the world, but primarily in the industrialised societies, use precious hours of their free time to go shopping. They have waited impatiently all week long for this free time while at work, usually earning less than they think they deserve. They enjoy this activity of shopping, which involves exchanging their hard-earned money for products of various sorts, most of which they do not really need and which they may soon ignore or discard after becoming bored with them. A day or two later, they go back to work to earn more money, to pay off credit card debts which they were lured into accumulating by tricky interest-rate advertising and even trickier product advertisements that promised power, sex, status, and happiness if only they can manage to possess these products. Meanwhile, they know very well that the manufacture of the products required to meet global demand and related waste-disposal problems are destroying their planet's ecosystems and enslaving another billion or two workers in sweatshops nearby and in the Third World.

To avoid getting into technical debates, we could call this ideological process *consumerism*. As we make this assertion several obvious questions must be addressed:

- What exactly in all this is ideology? What is indicated by this concept?
- Why is it important to theorise ideology? Why has psychology tended to ignore it?
- How can ideology best be theorised? What mode of interpretation is adequate to comprehend its nature?
- What is assumed to be the practical effect of ideology criticism? What forms of ideology criticism are likely to be worth pursuing?

What is ideology?

Unfortunately, it is still necessary to point out that the colloquial usage of ideology referring to a belief system about how the world should be organised is not especially helpful. It leads to endless debates about whose worldview is ideological and whose contains the truth. Contemporary *critical* definitions of ideology are related to the Marxist concept of false consciousness, but put less emphasis on the purely cognitive dimensions of the ideological process and more on its material and performative aspects. I concur with Thompson's general definition of ideology as a system of representations and practices that sustains and reproduces social relations characterised by oppression and domination.[2] For example, the ideological systems of sexism or racism include not only cognitive attitudes of prejudice, but also institutionalised discriminatory practices and exploitation and emotion-laden scripts that set up racist and sexist actions on the part of individuals and groups. Similarly, Kovel suggests that ideology consists of three interrelated processes at the individual, institutional, and discursive levels.[3]

The concept of ideology is thus necessarily broad in scope. It would include phenomena ranging from imperialism to rape and from capitalist wage- and salary-systems to the sexist childcare practices of a single day-care worker. Yet, it is specific in its attention to such phenomena in that it focuses on the flows of power, both destructive and productive, that simultaneously *hold oppressive systems in place by defusing or punishing resistance* and *produce eager new participants in social relations characterised by domination, exploitation, and coercion.*

Why is it important to theorise ideology?
Why has psychology ignored it?

Attempts to change social relations without an understanding of ideological processes tend to reproduce ideology, as the sad experience of many revolutionary governments teaches us. The path toward desirable change is thus not as clear as it may seem and any change-oriented action necessarily risks banking on certain aspects of the existing ideological process. This does not mean, as some neo-conservative postmodern theorists argue, that working for social change is always simply another form of blind participation in ideology. Instead, this possibility implies that an ongoing process of ideology criticism should accompany all practical efforts for change.

It may not be necessary to explain why psychology has ignored ideology. The case against dominant psychology has been made repeatedly over the last two decades and it seems that anyone who will hear and understand will have done so by now. Briefly, the primary modes of psychological theory, method, and practice are themselves intricately associated with the development of the individualism presupposed by liberal governments.[4] This individualism requires a notion of the human subject as autonomous and self-determining through rational choice. The concept of ideology implies that the states referred to as autonomy and self-determination are not givens, but instead are relatively rare *achievements*, given the fact that they depend on extended participation in forms of dialogue and solidarity that run counter to the social practices reinforced by the institutions of Western individualism. This is a different position from the one taken by Rose, which assumes, after Foucault, that autonomy is itself a fiction. In a sense, psychology has been a kind of limited software that fails to recognise the hardware on which it runs. Ironically, while its self-concept is that it is about the business of enlightenment through science, psychology's rampant individualism has reduced its practical impact to that of other ideology-machines such as advertising and the commercial news media.

How can ideology best be theorised?

This is one of the toughest questions and one in which theorists of ideology have been entangled for generations. The difficulty stems in part from disagreements about how ideology should be defined in the first place and about how it works, which is of course related to how it is defined. While these debates help to sharpen thinking, they have tended to be unnecessarily obscure and have contributed little to practical struggles.

For the purposes of these comments, it is most important to stress that the best theorising in relation to ideology will begin to destabilise ideology in the very process of theorising. This can happen through various practices that foster a *re-symbolisation of ideologised forms of life*. Here, the term re-symbolisation refers to a process that would partially overcome the fragmentation of affect, thought, and action that accompanies social practices characterised by domination.[5] It would effect a 'decolonisation' of the spaces in which subjective and collective meanings are produced and transformed. In the case of consumerism, for example, re-symbolisation would link the compulsion to buy unneeded products to the psychic suffering and practical limitations caused by indebtedness and to participation in the destructive globalisation of capital. Decolonisation might mean participation in co-ops, equipment sharing, and political work in solidarity with exploited workers around the world.

What sort of theorising would do this? Clearly, it would have to be socially engaged, not privatised, isolated work. It would be a process that reveals and challenges the connections between the different ideological moments: discourse, institution, and character. It would be a process that reproduces as little as possible the structures of power it challenges – thus, a questioning, ironic, negating, playfully serious mode. It would insist on radically democratic practice in the very process of understanding and questioning self, other, and social order. It would thus prefigure the forms of social being we would hope to foster.

Do we have examples of such de-ideologising practice? I would say that we can only point to bits and pieces here and there (which is the point of this programmatic manifesto in the first place!). We see some of these pieces in participatory action research, in the work of conscientisation associated with the ideas of Paolo Freire, in critical psychoanalytic life history research, in oral history studies with marginalised groups, in feminist research methods, in critical psychology approaches to community psychology, in solidarity work with psychiatric patients, and in Latin American liberation psychology.[6] Yet, in general, it is fair to say that the various modes of critical psychology, particularly its academic versions, have yet to achieve the aims associated with effective ideology criticism.

What might be the practical effects of ideology criticism?

There has been understandable resistance among ideology theorists to specify the potential long-term effects of ideology criticism. This resistance stems from an insistence that citizens engaged in democratic processes should themselves be the ones to determine social goals. Nevertheless, the sorts of ends that could be realistically expected to follow from a sustained process of ideology criticism would include:

- the expansion of forms of living in accordance with deeply felt needs and meanings, articulated in fully participatory democratic processes,
- the reduction of automatic submission (and compulsive reaction) to domination,
- increased availability of collective social spaces not directly mediated by market and state pressures to achieve status through prescribed actions, and
- rearrangement of political and economic structures flowing from the deepening of democracy.

What are the limits of the practice of ideology criticism?

It may sound as if ideology criticism is nothing less than an academic, intellectualised moment of radical citizenship or a description of what academics can do to contribute to emancipatory politics. There is quite a bit of truth in this, but ideology criticism also requires significant commitments to scholarship grounded in both everyday experience and global awareness. The primary difference between ideology criticism and traditional scholarship would be the degree to which the impulse, the purpose, and the effects of the work are connected to social movements rather than one's personal academic fancies.

A version of these comments was presented at the 1999 conference of the International Society for Theoretical Psychology in Sydney.

Notes

1. Cf. E. Sampson, *Celebrating the Other: A Dialogic Account of Human Nature*, Harvester Wheatsheaf, London 1993; W.R. Earnest, 'Ideology Criticism and Interview Research', in G. Rosenwald and R. Ochberg (eds), *Storied Lives*, Yale University Press, New Haven 1992, pp250-264.
2. J. Thompson, *Studies in the Theory of Ideology*, University of California Press, Berkeley 1984.
3. J. Kovel, 'On Racism and Psychoanalysis', in S. Frosh and A. Elliott (eds), *Psychoanalysis in Contexts*, Routledge, London 1995, pp205-222.
4. N. Rose, *Inventing our Selves: Psychology, Power, and Personhood*, Cambridge University Press, London 1998.
5. Cf. T. Sloan, *Damaged Life: The Crisis of the Modern Psyche*, Routledge, London 1996.
6. Cf. D. Fox and I. Prilleltensky (eds), *Critical Psychology: An Introduction*, Sage, London 1997; I. Parker, 'Critical Psychology: Critical Links', *Annual Review of Critical Psychology*, 1, 1999, pp3-18; T. Sloan (ed), *Critical Psychology: Voices for Change*, Macmillan, London 2000.

Reviews

Kenneth J. Gergen, An Invitation to Social Construction
Sage, 1999

David J. Nightingale and John Crombie (eds), Social Constructionist Psychology: A Critical Analysis of Theory and Practice
Open University Press, 1999

Nikki Parker

Social constructionist psychology: is there something missing?

These are two quite contrasting books on social constructionism (SC). Gergen's is an authored text, an exciting and lucid introduction to SC written by its most prominent exponent. Nightingale and Crombie's book (N&C) is an edited collection of critical articles which more or less adopt the editors' central aim to 'loosen the focus' on discourse within SC.

Nightingale and Crombie's book is part of a trilogy of critical reviews of social constructionist perspectives in psychology. The others in the series are Parker et al.'s *Critical Textwork,* on methodological issues in discourse analysis (DA), and Willig's *Applied Discourse Analysis*, which is a set of discussions on how DA can be applied as a research tool. N&C are positioned alongside these other two by taking a step back to review the broader picture of SC as a theoretical perspective within which DA sits. The book's title seems to promise an overview or exposition of SC and its psychological applications. However it turns out to be more a critique than an exposition, and its subtitle is a better indicator of its contents. The editors declare themselves 'broadly sympathetic to social constructionism' (pxv), but their main concern is to elaborate its shortcomings, in particular SC's overemphasis on the linguistic. To redress the balance N&C promote the (re)introduction of their central concerns, which are the issues of embodiment, materiality and power, to which are linked various other worries, for example SC's 'refus[al] to theorise the self' (p146) and its lack of 'a description of the person' (p152).

The key objective for N&C is to highlight the ways in which these aspects are 'missing' from SC, and to explore how they might be successfully incorporated. The main issue in seeking to evaluate this endeavour is to consider the plausibility of attempting to include them within SC's explanatory terms of reference rather than as they currently stand, as topics for discursive analysis. The authors set themselves the challenge of creating a way of theorising these and other 'problems' which can embrace 'both the "real" *and* the "constructed"' (p15), a challenge which of itself I would say is questionable as an attainable goal. These positions are less like two different colours of paint that can easily be blended to produce a new hue, and more like oil and water, which are basically incompatible materials.

The middle section of N&C, on materiality and embodiment, contains the real 'guts' of the argument proposed: six chapters tackling 'the self', 'realism', 'embodiment' and the 'extra-discursive'. Some are argued more clearly than others, with one or two displaying a rather muddled portrayal of the concepts which they attempt to refute. Ian Burkett focuses particularly on the ways in which power, language and practice are embedded within social relations. Following Kurt Danzinger, he explores the possibility of two kinds of SC, the 'light' and the 'dark'. In the light version, 'life is constructed in discourse and power is embedded in that medium' (p69) whereas the dark version sees discourse as 'embedded in relations of power that form systems of constraint which regulate social actions' (ibid.). What Burkett seems to be suggesting is that we try to find a way of theorising a twilight zone between the two which will neuter the dangerous extremes of either position. However, the distinctions between light and dark as he defines them may well be so polarised as not actually to be best thought of as part of the same continuum. Maybe we should instead recognise several different and opposed approaches to language and reality that have so far loosely and misleadingly been labelled SC, rather than struggling with an assumption that the term 'social constructionism' as it is so diversely appropriated, is a single entity requiring integration.

Part three of N&C makes the move towards a 'critical analysis of practice' with contributions by Erica Burman, Christine Henwood and Wendy and Rex Stainton Rogers. Burman takes a feminist standpoint in tackling the issue of 'what is at stake' in the recent moves from SC to deconstruction and on toward reconstruction in psychology. The difficulty for anyone with a clear political objective is that, in order to change society, one has to show that it is a certain way to begin with. While SC may initially have been welcomed by critical psychologists as providing a way of de-stabilising prevailing notions of social and psychological reality, and useful in demonstrating the constructed nature of relationships and notions of the self, those who embraced it in that manner as a critical weapon have subsequently perhaps realised that it is a double-edged sword. The problem with taking SC seriously is that one has to accept that it can and perhaps ought to be applied to all arenas of discourse, including one's own. The threat of having the rug pulled from under one's feet seems to be the point at which elements of 'realism' are being brought back in. However, preserving some realities as more real than others, or as pre-existing or beyond the scope of critical SC, seems unworkable and inconsistent. This move forwards to 'reconstruction', as it is framed in N&C, seems more like a retreat from SC, and it leads us back to the very same problems of facticity, reality and description that gave rise to it in the first place.

Gergen's is a particularly authoritative text, given his founding status in SC, but its authority is tempered by his offering it in the form of an 'invitation'. Coupled with the engaging clarity of the writing, it is likely to be valuable not only as a coherent introduction or teaching text, but also as a resource for seasoned practitioners, who will benefit from its refreshing and erudite vision of the enterprise in which they are engaged. Despite its 'invitational' stance, it is a sophisticated treatment of sometimes difficult and challenging arguments. It is beautifully written and probably as accessible as it could be, while retaining its seriousness. The overall style and structure of the book is approachable and thoughtfully laid-out, with each chapter finishing with helpful but concise pointers for further reading on each of the topics within.

The term 'invitation' in Gergen's title echoes Berger's celebrated *Invitation to Sociology*, [1] which in turn echoes Berger & Luckmann's *Social Construction of Reality*, [2] one of SC's inspirational texts. Gergen's own invitation is addressed personally to the reader, with further echoes of Barthes and the semioticians, to co-author the text through engaging actively with it in the process of reading. In this gentle but persuasive manner, Gergen not only writes *about* SC but simultaneously engages *in* it, providing the reader with enough open-ended arguments and resources to make that invitation not just another persuasive trope, but a truly irresistible enticement.

In Gergen's SC, the concept of persons as essentially individual selves with cognitive processes and self determination, is replaced with a notion of the 'relational being'. [3] As with postmodernism, SC is offered not merely as an interesting new way of thinking about ourselves, a new theory of the same object, but as an observation on historical, social and intellectual changes that are already happening. So it is an invitation not just to a new set of ideas, but to a new way to live your life. It is real lives and principles for living them that N&C find missing from SC: The question is whether that observation does justice to SC. Gergen would claim not. Without shirking these concerns, he focuses critically on SC's major psychological target, the Cartesian foundation of mainstream psychology and of our major social institutions, the concept of individual selves, possessed of private minds and their problematic relations to an objectively-knowable external reality. Along with Wittgenstein and Rorty, he does not propose a solution to the ancient problems of knowledge and agency that begin from that 'self' conception but, rather, suggests we set them aside as unnecessary metaphors. The 'invitation' is not just to intellectual thinking and epistemic debate, but to actually engage with life's problems, geared to the reduction of conflict and oppression. Gergen is concerned with real lives, and with social as well as epistemic transformation: 'deliberating on our common discourses – in science and everyday life – can have liberating consequences. Critique gives way to emancipation and creative construction of alternatives' (p5). [4] Whereas a liberal humanist might view such an open and democratic future hopefully, there remains scope for alternative constructions, not only of outcomes but of the forces that shape them – the kind of sensibility evident in many of the contributions to N&C, and often ranged against constructionism. It is as if our political landscape really were created in discussions and debating chambers. SC's response is that any such notions of economic and structural constraints are not ignored, but figure as the stuff of discourse and rhetoric, backed by evidence and factual descriptions.

Gergen confronts the main objection to SC and related discourse-based approaches: that their prime concern with language ignores the non-linguistic, by which is meant the material world, our engagement in it, and subjective experience of it. The force of that objection is weakened once we let go of its underlying 'picture theory' of language as representations of life, while actual life goes on in other, more basic domains. Gergen's SC is founded in an appreciation of discourse itself as forms of life, forms of practical action, within which the nature of the world beyond language is constructed and acted on. Indeed, it is the work of discourse, and representational practices generally, to 'essentialise' their referents (p45),[5] to render factual and real the very objects that are then promoted by critics of SC as lying beyond the reach of discursive and constructionist analysis.

Gergen discusses critical issues and objections made against SC not just by producing a series of arguments and refutations but rather by showing how SC can approach and deal with such matters, sometimes without obligation to provide straightforward or definitive answers. That is not merely because definitive answers are lacking, but because providing them would endorse the terms of reference in which the objections are made, and SC is radical enough to imply different ways of asking as well as of answering questions. For example, there is the issue of whether experience or agency is, in some sense, prior to and beyond the reach of SC. Gergen argues, with echoes now of Wittgenstein, that these are 'simply questions that do not require answers. The more important question for the constructionist concerns the consequences … of placing such terms into motion' (p225). It is, of course, SC's prerogative, as in the related domains of discursive and rhetorical psychology, not to have to come up with definitive answers or final resolutions but, rather, to celebrate debate and tension as productive, open-ended modes of knowledge and reasoning.

But does SC deny what is obvious and real and outside of language

– bodies, death, pollution, and so on? Gergen claims that such objections are 'based on a misunderstanding of constructionist arguments … constructionism doesn't try to rule on what is or is not fundamentally real. Whatever is, simply is. However, *the moment we begin to articulate* what there is … we enter a world of discourse, and thus a tradition, a way of life, and a set of value preferences' (p222, emphasis added).[6] In SC, discourse is not merely words and descriptions, while the nature of the 'real' world lies beyond it. Discourse is not language, but practices of description, narrative, rhetoric – practices in which the nature of the world, of bodily experience, materiality, is formulated. SC's argument is that those practices (common-sense descriptions, science, the writing of history, etc.) are themselves the ways in which we construct and decide upon the nature of things. It is not a matter of denying the existence of a world beyond words, but of denying its role as independent arbiter of the truth of descriptions. As Gergen puts it, 'the terms by which we understand our world and our self are neither required nor demanded by "what there is"' (p47). Except to say, of course, that producing one's descriptions *as* 'demanded by what there is', as science does, and court rooms, and classrooms, and everyday event reporting, is the best way to be convincing.

Let us return therefore to the major issue for N&C: what is social constructionism, and can it be productively amended in the way that book argues? Some clarification of terms of reference would help. Gergen provides a useful set of distinctions between various similar-looking notions used in psychology, including importantly those between social constructivism (with a 'v') and social constructionism (SC). According to Gergen, SC has 'a primary emphasis on discourse' (p60). But it is precisely the centrality of discourse in SC, offered by Gergen as *its defining feature*, that N&C find inadequate. The way in which that inadequacy is declared involves making a series of glosses on SC that set it up for criticism. A prime target of critical comment by Nightingale and Crombie, in both their introduction and their concluding chapter, is the anti-realism article 'Death and furniture' by Edwards, Ashmore and Potter,[7] which lurks in the background of the book like a ghost at a wedding, present in spirit but not in body. Given the centrality of the 'discourse' argument to SC and its critique, it is unhelpful to have it represented only indirectly in this way via quotes, glosses and refutations, rather than actually present and argued. In contrast, a related volume by Parker includes a defence by Potter which provides this kind of balance that, which N&C lacks.[8]

The 'absence' from N&C of a clear case for what Gergen defines as the essence of SC means that much of the argument against it takes the form of unopposed denials and contradictions. For example, 'the idea that we can always be (radically) sceptical of every aspect of reality cannot be maintained' (N&C, 216). It is hard to disagree, but one has to ask, is that in fact SC's position? Does anybody actually propose that we *can* 'always' be sceptical of 'every' aspect of reality? What SC argues is not that constant scepticism is always possible on all fronts at once, but rather, that no 'aspect of reality', however committed to it we are, is immune from or prior to the same kind of analysis that we apply to whatever truths we may favour.

The idea that SC psychology lacks a theory of the self, or requires a principle of non-discursive embodiment, is really to mistake what SC is distinctively about. Its central claim is not that the objects of those words have no external reality, but that it is a futile enterprise to invoke it as any kind of independent criterion for the adequacy of descriptions. Much of the effort of SC, and of discursive psychology,[9] is aimed precisely at how notions of a non-discursive domain of factual reality are discursively produced. This is not to deny the usefulness for psychology of a notion such as embodiment, which has much to recommend it, nor to deny the existence of bodies and experiences, but rather, it is an objection to the idea that SC lacks such notions and needs to incorporate them, not as topics but as part of SC's explanatory terms of reference. I see such a move as one that can only confuse and obscure what SC is 'essentially' all about rather than improve it. Such theorising would be better served if it simply called itself by a different name.

Notes

1. P. Berger, *An Invitation to Sociology*. Anchor Books, New York 1963.
2. P. Berger & T. Luckmann, *The Social Construction of Reality*, Doubleday, Garden City 1966.
3. Cf. R. Harré, *Personal Being: A Theory for Individual Psychology*, Blackwell, Oxford 1983; J. Shotter, *Conversational Realities: Constructing Life Through Language*, Sage, London 1993.
4. Cf. M. Billig, S. Condor, D. Edwards, M. Gane, D.J. Middleton, & A.R. Radley, *Ideological Dilemmas: A Social Psychology of Everyday Thinking*, Sage, London 1988, p5.

5. Cf. J. Potter, *Representing Reality: Discourse, Rhetoric, and Social Construction*, Sage, London 1996.
6. Cf. D. Edwards, M. Ashmore & J. Potter, 'Death and Furniture: The Rhetoric, Politics, and Theology of Bottom Line Arguments Against Relativism', *History of the Human Sciences, 8* (2), 1995, pp25-49.
7. *Ibid.*
8. J. Potter, 'Fragments in the Realization of Relativism', in I. Parker (ed) *Social Constructionism, Discourse and Realism*, Sage, London 1998.
9. For example D. Edwards & J. Potter, *Discursive Psychology*, Sage, London 1992; J. Potter, 1996, *op. cit.*

Ángel J. Gordo-López and Ian Parker (eds), Cyberpsychology

Macmillan Press, Basingstoke 1999, (ISBN 0333735773 (pbk))

Elaine Lally

This edited collection addresses important contemporary cultural and intellectual questions of technology and the self, questions which cross disciplinary boundaries and are of interest to philosophers of technology and cultural theorists as well as psychologists. Like me, for many readers this book will be their first introduction to 'cyberpsychology'. Given the nature of the intellectual project undertaken in *Cyberpsychology*, it would perhaps be surprising if the book managed to present a consistent whole picture. Indeed it does not, and each reader will find in the volume something different. For me, the book provided rich material for developing post-Cartesian understandings of the self in relation to technology. While in classical terms, subjects and objects were seen as bounded and monadic natural entities interacting in Newtonian fashion, it has now become clear that the subject-object relation may be better envisaged as a dynamic interface with complex topology. A simplistic mind-body distinction is impossible to maintain in exploring the relationship of the self to the Internet and other contemporary communication and information technologies. Further, because technologies are formed within and implicated in the maintenance of large-scale socio-technical systems and have a particularly close implication in processes of globalisation, it is also impossible to ignore questions of power and social and economic relations.

For the editors and contributors to this collection, the 'cyber' in cyberpsychology is both the cyber of cyberspace and the cyber in cyborg. The most interesting contributions, for me at least, are those which explore the possibilities for cyberspatialised selves – spatially and temporally distributed, complex technologically- and culturally-embedded selves – rather than those in which the self in cyberpsychology is a technologically hybridised 'cyborged' self. As Nightingale points out in her commentary piece, there is a definite anthropomorphism to the cyborg envisaged as simply a prostheticised human. Erica Burman's contribution, for example, explores how both the child and the cyborg have been used to inspire and personify visions of the future, forming 'key cultural repositories for the repressed fears and fantasies to which modern subjectivity gives rise' (p169). Dan Heggs, in examining the relation of the cyborg to super-hero narratives, proposes that it is possible to reconfigure the super-hero and the cyborg through moving the emphasis away from the analysis of identity to that of reporting events. In this way, Heggs suggests, it becomes possible to find new vantage points for an examination of various forms of domination and transgression. The cyborg is a central image and concept within cyberpsychology because 'it is the site, the "body", that can be made legible and can be thought of as the starting-point for explorations of the relationships between humans and technology' (p185). The danger in anthropomorphism, as Heggs is clearly aware, is that 'of naturalisation and reclamation, particularly when the focus is placed on the individual body' (p192-193).

This is an anxiety which runs throughout this volume. 'Cyberpsychology' explicitly defines its intellectual project in opposition to more traditional forms of psychological enquiry. As the editors point out in their introduction, while the mind has been compared to different kinds of technology since antiquity, these analogies have more often than not found themselves conscripted into the service of dominant economic and political structures. In particular, through the combination of cybernetics and cognitive psychology, psychology has progressively moved from being a science of prediction and control to becoming one of the important controlling sciences (p2-3).

For the editors and contributors to this collection, there is a very real danger that developing understandings of the self in the contemporary technological context will again be co-opted to serve reactionary rather than progressive political interests. The editors ask whether:

> cyberspace, and the different forms of subjectivity that inhabit it, poses a challenge, or not, to technologies of surveillance and control which comprise the modern 'psy-techno complex', which we define as the dense network of virtual and material technologies and practices to do with the 'mind' and 'behaviour' that comprise academic and professional work and psychology inside and outside the classroom and the clinic in popular culture (p6).

Contemporary understandings of identity as flexible and multiple, for example, may find themselves serving the needs of workplace managers in new conditions of flexible knowledge production, just as they are already shaping the strategies of marketers and advertisers. Cyberpsychology is part of wider psychological culture, including popular understandings of psychological phenomena. An increasingly educated and sophisticated public already provides an ever-expanding market for commodified forms of academic knowledge, including the proliferation of democratising fictions of the Internet as opening access for all to information.

Despite the expressed wish on the part of this collection's editors that cyberpsychology should not be something to be absorbed into the mainstream in this way, it is not at all clear how this might be avoided or even that it is possible at all. The following provocative statement, for example, appears to suggest a form of guerrilla hyper-criticality as a strategy of intellectual resistance:

> To avoid such psychological enframing of cyberpsychology, then, we have to be able to devise ways of articulating its own death. That is, cyberpsy-

chology needs to embed within itself a self-annihilating device, a certain kind of critical and self-critical narrative which both helps it to resist incorporation into the discipline and, at the moment it is incorporated, to go critical and explode inside the discipline causing the maximum amount of damage. Think of it as containing a highly sensitive critical clock mechanism which is triggered when it finds itself being published in mainstream books and journals and becoming part of the social scientific and psychological spectacle. You are reading this already. Is this the time? We want to insist that it is only in its *ephemeral* use that the potential of cyberpsychological critique can function, that it will be able to be the deconstructive spanner in the machinery of the psy-techno complex (p16).

To avoid becoming disciplined, then, cyberpsychology must be more than just an *inter*-discipline. It must actively become an *anti*-discipline. Just as bringing together matter and anti-matter results in their mutual annihilation, so too, should cyberpsychology and the mainstream, if brought into sufficiently close proximity. As the editors recognise, the book's very existence objectifies and gives closure to one particular set of statements about what cyberpsychology 'is'. It is published by a mainstream publisher and can be found on Amazon.com. Here it is being reviewed in an international refereed journal. One can't help but wonder if the editors' insistence that cyberpsychological critique should be ephemeral might have been better served in a more intrinsically ephemeral mode – perhaps even as an electronic publication.

The intellectual project of *Cyberpsychology* therefore emerges out of an expressly political commitment on the part of many of the contributors to the book. But while this is articulated with some theoretical sophistication within the collection, examples of what such a politics would actually look like in everyday praxis are only developed to a limited degree. Cromby and Standen's contribution, for example, deploys the notion of subjective possibility spaces to provide a way of assessing the impact of cyberspace and related technologies on the subjectivity of people with disabilities. The authors suggest that these technologies may open up possibilities for people with disabilities or close them down, and come to the inevitable conclusion that technologies often do both at the same time. A house designed for people with disabilities, for example, may be equipped with equipment which can alert care-staff if a potential problem is detected. While such a house would give a disabled inhabi-

tant the security of knowing that they had protection from the consequences of accidents and crises, it would also clearly mean inhabiting an
environment which involves continual, if passive, surveillance. These
considerations would undoubtedly have a complex influence on the subjectivity of the inhabitant. While this paper provides a starting-point,
then, towards exploring the effect on subjectivity of changing possibility
spaces, more work needs to be done in order to understand the profound
and complex ambivalence these inevitably engender.

Other authors in the collection follow up in theoretical terms how
the ambivalence of the prosthetic in the increasingly integrated and
interdependent relationship between humans and their technologies
arises. James Sey traces this issue via a historical analysis of the body-
technology relation and subjectivity in Taylorism and since. The
integration between the embodied human worker and technology
within Taylorism results in a dehumanising of the worker, who is essentially a prosthesis of the machine. In the postmodern moment the
human re-emerges from this identification with the machine into a new
era when subjectivity is re-asserted, the body-machine relation is
inverted, and technology is naturalised into the subjective environment.
Via a consideration of the psychogenesis of the technological relationship, Carlos Soldevilla Pérez proposes a psychoanalytic understanding
of technique as an effect of the irrepressible unfolding of human desire
for omnipotence, expressing a perverse narcissism. Betty M. Bayer
explores struggles over meaning-making and boundary-making around
what counts as human, and suggests that 'technovisions … are less
about settling issues of who we are than struggles over *kinds* of bodies-,
selves-, and worlds-in-the-making' (p126).

This is the conceptual point at which this collection extends notions
of the cyber-self beyond anthropomorphic cyborg visions and into the
realm of complex topologies of the self in relation to technology.
Nightingale imagines media flows, for example, as cyborg entities
which are 'dependent on transitory appropriations of human bodies
and other physical and psychological properties of humans for their
existence … [borrowing] human qualities by enticing humans into
their flowing' (p228). Heidi J. Figueroa-Sarriera suggests, via an exploration of MUD interaction, a conceptualisation of the subject as a
complex communication network, with the body as an apparatus with
a wireless connection to an electronic communication network.

Figueroa-Sarriera thus evokes Virilio's metaphor of a 'terminal' existence (which was referred to earlier in the volume by Sey) in the double sense of being at an 'end', but also connected to the 'network'. The subject is at the same time both embodied and spatially distributed: 'the embodied subject transmutes – that is, changes, in transit, into a disembodied subject – only partially and temporarily' (p141). The social and technological context of interaction provides the psychological conditions for the development of the subject, because it incorporates a self-reference apparatus which facilitates self-reflexivity.

As Steve Jones points out, McLuhan's characterisation of communication media as extensions of man was meant to make sense in the realm of the senses. The Internet as prosthesis, however, is less an extension of our senses than an extension of our selves. Francisco Javier Tirado explores the morphology of such an extended self. This is a self which resists description in terms of the dominant conceptual model for intellectual categories in Western traditions of academic thought, that of constant, stable and consistent entities with distinct and distinguishable borders. What it requires are models which introduce 'oscillation between frontiers, shaking around the edges, borders with mobility and flexibility' (p204). Tirado, following Serres, suggests that the flame might be a more appropriate model for such concepts:

> The topology of a flame is extremely paradoxical. The edges of the flame vary at such a speed for us that it is impossible to say either if they are actually present or where they are … It continues and it discontinues. It is more than unstable and less than stable. It is not a flow, as it lacks any constant to give it order. It is random fluctuation, always the same flame but bearing no relation to what it was a moment ago … It has no constant edges, frontiers or margins. The flame enables us to get away from representationalist thinking (p205).

The logic of the flame is taken up by Tirado through Deleuze and Guattari's notion of becoming. The cyborg is a becoming in this sense: it is 'a movement of endless incorporation … [W]e become mixtures at the intersection of animal and machine … [T]hese mixtures are not constant but change repeatedly [in an] agonising process, without origins or teleologies' (p206).

A description of such a cyborg is given by Jill Marsden through a cyberpsychological reading of Judge Schreber's autobiographical work, *Memoirs of My Nervous Illness* (1903). Marsden argues that Freud's analysis of Schreber's feminisation simply confirms the prejudices of traditional psychology. Schreber's intensely psychotic delusional systems are reduced to a case of Oedipal conflict through a commitment to 'hierarchical, centralised control structures which relentlessly situate the Schreberian fantasia within the locus of the family and relations of affiliation' (p65). Marsden argues, on the contrary, that within Schreber's work can be read 'a philosophy of communication which extends the boundaries of Schreber's body into a vast network of connection beyond all familiar socio-temporal co-ordinates and species boundaries' (p61). Schreber's transformation is realised in terms of its material engagements: this is an autoerotic affectivity 'sprung loose from biological finality' which has 'nothing to do with lack, negation or loss, rather it institutes an explosion of sexuality as materially emergent' (p70).

Marsden suggests that the view of the embodied subject 'as an emergent system within webs of integration' poses a serious challenge 'to the Freudian technologies of surveillance and control that compose the psy-complex' (p72). This returns us both to the central intellectual and political project of *Cyberpsychology* and to its anxiety about conservative mainstream co-option. Marsden wonders whether there is indeed any benefit to women from such a theory of the postbiological body or whether it is just another postmodern 'idealization of the feminine as metaphor for the chaotic, the fluid and the irrational' (p72).

Both Marsden's contribution and that of Steven D. Brown are the highlights of the volume for me. Brown's contribution, in particular, brings together and philosophically synthesises the central issues raised throughout the collection. Brown explores the cyborg as transhuman: 'spawned by the convergence of technics with "meat", the transhuman is a creature that lives somewhere between our notions of the natural and the artificial, the real and the virtual' (p149). The transhuman is, however, literally monstrous, a category error which threatens to undo all existing categories and divisions.

Brown points out that it is our technologies that have made us what we are: 'technics hold us together' (p154). The naturalisation of technology into the subjective environment, traced historically by Sey, is experienced, according to Brown, as the consumption – even harvesting – of the human subject by electronic technologies. Almost by definition, the cyborg is that which retains the ability to 'keep it all together' under these postmodern conditions. How it is that we can hold it all together in the face of our transhuman monstrosity implies a knowledge of what the technology of cyberspace really *is*, in its essence. This cannot be known *a priori* about technologies, but rather is precisely what is most at stake in historical debates about the emergence of new technologies. The management of such monstrosity is a matter of *social* technics.

Brown draws on Heidegger in elaborating the issue of the essence of the contemporary technological environment, and suggests that the anxiety and the profound ambivalence which accompany transhumanism arise because:

> it is technology which engenders monstrosity by 'unconcealing' things which would otherwise not be brought about, the most monstrous of which is the way in which we come to recognise ourselves as simple resources at our own disposal ... [Yet] our means of dealing with monstrosity is then precisely the same practice that results in its emergence in the first place. Thus the only way that we can possibly continue to hold it all together is to drive ever harder onwards as *technikos*, beings in the sway of *technikon* (p159).

To live in this way it to live in perpetual anxiety. But it is a productive anxiety since it forces us to confront the dialectic of intimacy and alienation which marks out modern technics. Brown's contribution shows how Heidegger gives us a

> rich vocabulary for talking about this movement between anxiety and security. We can speak of the relationship between humans and technology not as an 'interaction', an 'impact' or any other of the terms which reify the cognitive subject, but as a matter of *placing*, an ordering of humans and machines all mixed up together (p162).

The ambitious scope of *Cyberpsychology* inevitably means that many more very interesting and important questions are raised than are answered. However, the varied contributions do provide a variety of directions for further exploration of humans and technologies all mixed up together.

Notes on contributors

Sybil Ahmane has been both a user of psychiatric services and a mental health worker. She now co-runs an experiential and visual training package for mental health professionals called Learning from Psychosis. Website: www.learningfrompsychosis.com

Stephanie Austin is a doctoral student at York University. After having completed her MA in Community Psychology at Wilfrid Laurier University, she decided to pursue her studies in Critical Psychology in the history and theory of psychology programme at York. Stephanie is particularly interested in equity studies (e.g., feminism and anti-racism) in psychology. She can be reached at saustin@yorku.ca

Benjamin Bradley is currently head of psychology at Charles Sturt University, where he is co-leading the development of a more experience-based pedagogy in the psychology curriculum. He is a member of CSU's Centre for Cultural Research into Risk, for which he is spearheading an action-research 'Living at Risk' project with those living at risk in Bathurst. His first contact with critical psychology was through the Centre for Child Care and Development at Cambridge University during the early 1980s. In 1989 he published *Visions of Infancy: A Critical Introduction to Child Psychology* (Polity Press, also available in French, Spanish and Italian). With William Kessen, he co-edited a Special Issue of *Theory & Psychology* on The Future of Developmental Theory (1993). He now conducts observational research on early intersubjectivity in groups of babies during the first year of life (with Jane

Selby), is researching the relation between domestic and public discourse in the unpublished correspondence of William James and is studying the links between depression during pregnancy with postnatal depression with Reinhold Muller and Barbara Hayes. He currently holds an ARC grant to study forms of ethical reasoning surrounding the 'Harms of Heroin' with Steve James and Seumas Miller.

Michelle Fine is a Professor of social/personality psychology at the Graduate School and University Centre, City University of New York. Her recent books include: *Constriction Sites: Spaces for and by Urban Youth* (with Lois Weis, Teachers College Press, 2000), and *Speedbumps: A Student Friendly Guide to the Politics and Methods of Qualitative Research* (with Lois Weis, Teachers College Press, 2000).

Russell Hall completed a BA(hons) degree in communication Studies and Film History in 1996 at the University of East London. His Masters Degree, in Film and Video, at The London Institute was completed in 1999 and he now teaches Media Studies at Redbridge College, London.

Dr Arnd Hofmeister is a lecturer in the Institute for Critical Psychology, Free University of Berlin. He has published widely in the areas of theoretical and educational Psychology. His research interests include Critical Psychologies, Poststructuralism, Discourse-analysis, and Queer-Theory. Arnd is currently conducting research on societalisation, societal transformation and embodiment.

Wendy Hollway is Professor and Head of Psychology at the Open University, UK. She has published in gender, sexuality and subjectivity, mothering, qualitative method, organisational psychology and fear of crime. Her latest book, with Tony Jefferson, is *Doing Qualitative Research Differently: Free Association, Narrative and the Interview Method* (Sage, London 2000).

Alexander Kouzmin holds the Foundation Chair in Management in the Graduate School of Management at the University of Western Sydney, Australia. His research interests include organisational design; technological change; project management; comparative management;

administrative reform; and crisis management. He has published eight volumes of commissioned work. Among these are his edited *Public Sector Administration: Newer Perspectives* (Longman, Cheshire 1983); his co-edited (with N. Scott,) *Dynamics in Australian Public Management: Selected Essays* (Macmillan, 1990); (with L. Still, P. and Clarke) *New Directions in Management* (McGraw Hill, 1994); (with J. Garnett,) *Handbook of Administrative Communication* (Marcel Dekker, 1997); and (with A. Hayne,) *Essays in Economic Globalization, Transnational Policies and Vulnerability* (IIAS, 1999, forthcoming). He has contributed chapters to many national and international volumes and has published some 150 papers, including scholarly and review articles in more than 40 leading international refereed journals. He is on the editorial board of *Administration and Society; Administrative Theory and Praxis; International Journal of Management History; Journal of Management Development; Journal of Public Administration and Management: An Interactive Journal; Journal of Public Affairs Education; Public Policy and Administration; Public Productivity and Management Review;* and *Public Voices*, and is a founding co-editor of the international *Journal of Contingencies and Crisis Management*, published quarterly since 1993.

Elaine Lally is a researcher and administrator with the Institute for Cultural Research, based at the University of Western Sydney. Elaine's research interests are focused around how people and the objects of the cultural environment mutually construct each other. Her PhD research, completed in 2000, was a study of home computer ownership which situated this technology as an item of domestic material culture, embedded in the dynamic patterns of everyday life.

Kareen Ror Malone is Associate Professor of Psychology and Women's Studies faculty at State University of West Georgia, USA. She has recently co-edited a text, *The Subject of Lacan: A Lacanian Reader for Psychology* (State University of New York).

Nikki Parker is a postgraduate researcher in the Department of Social Sciences, Loughborough University. Her research interests include the psychology of family relationships and therapeutic environments. Nikki is currently conducting research on institutional and mundane authority.

Professor Isaac Prilleltensky is the new Chair in the Department of Psychology at Victoria University in Melbourne, Australia. He is interested in emancipatory approaches in psychology and in promoting critical psychology praxis. He is currently collaborating with Professor Geoff Nelson from Wilfrid Laurier University on two books on applied critical psychology and community psychology and liberation (Macmillan Press).

Rosemarie Roberts is a doctoral candidate in the social/personality psychology programme, City University of New York, a dancer of Afro-Caribbean dance and a scholar of domination and resistance, particularly as manifested through Black dance in the Americas.

Tod Sloan is Associate Professor and Chair in the Department of Psychology at the University of Tulsa (Oklahoma), where he also directs a Centre for Community Research and Development. He is the author of *Damaged Life: The Crisis of the Modern Psyche* (Routledge, 1996) and editor of *Critical Psychology: Voices for Change* (Macmillan, 2000). He is currently working on *Critical Psychology: A Brief Critical Introduction*. In his other life, he is a co-parenting father, a Green Party activist, and a mediocre folk-rocker.

Maria Elena Torre is a doctoral candidate in the social/personality psychology programme at the Graduate Centre, City University of New York, and is an activist scholar involved with questions of incarceration of women, higher education and youth organising.

Debora Upegui is a doctoral candidate in the social/personality psychology programme at the Graduate School and University Center, City University of New York, and is interested in questions of language and the politics of language use and meaning.

Margaret H. Vickers is a Lecturer in the Graduate School of Management, University of Western Sydney, Australia. Prior to working at the University of Western Sydney-Nepean, she lectured at the University of Western Sydney-Hawkesbury and at the Australian Graduate School of Police Management, a faculty of Charles Sturt University. She has also previously lectured in computing at the

University of Western Sydney – Nepean. Margaret's eclectic research interests now span: management and organisation theory; trauma in organisations; qualitative research methodologies; organisational behaviour and communication; sociology of health and illness; workplace illness and disability; and the social and organisational aspects of information technology usage. In addition to her PhD in Management, Margaret also holds a Bachelor of Business in Computing and Information Systems and a Master of Business Administration (MBA), specialising in Management and Organisational Behaviour. She has published numerous articles and chapters in international refereed journals and volumes, and is on the executive of the US Association on Employment Practices and Principles.

ANNUAL REVIEW OF CRITICAL PSYCHOLOGY

~Action Research~

The second issue of *Annual Review of Critical Psychology* is a themed special Issue on **'Action Research'**. It will provide a forum to discuss ways of changing the world through varieties of action research, and to critically reflect on how psychology needs to change to be up to the task. By action research we mean a range of critical practical-theoretical interventions which include conscientization, cultural destabilisation, education inclusion campaigns, feminist research, mental health intervention, practical deconstruction and radical therapeutic activities. This special issue includes articles and reviews by writers in Canada, Colombia, Denmark, Mexico, Portugal, South Africa, Spain, the United Kingdom and Venezuela on issues including: gender and cultural resistance, disability research, the psychologisation of critical psychology, community theatre and political participation.

ARCP is an international refereed journal, providing an opportunity for readers to learn about theoretical frameworks and practical initiatives around the world. The first issue, which is still available, was published in July 1999 on the theme of **'Foundations'**.

Further subscription details from:

> Ian Parker, Discourse Unit,
> Department of Psychology and Speech Pathology,
> The Manchester Metropolitan University,
> Hathersage Road, Manchester,
> M13 OJA, UK.
> E-mail: I.A.Parker@mmu.ac.uk

Special offer to Critical Psychology readers

Buy new books direct from L&W, post-free and at discounted prices

This month's special offers are Timothy Bewes and Jeremy Gilbert's *Cultural Capitalism: Politics after New Labour* and Wendy Wheeler's *The Political Subject: Essays on the Self from Art, Politics and Science*

Cultural Capitalism
Politics after New Labour
edited by Timothy Bewes and Jeremy Gilbert

Cultural Capitalism presents a series of differing inflections of the contemporary relationship between politics and culture, at a time when the cultural domain is more than ever being seen as crucial to any political project. The contributors focus particularly on the cultural politics of New Labour, including its relationship to discourses of managerialism, its fascination with *grands projets*, and its self-mythologising investment in the concept of spin. There is also a section dealing with the state of interdisciplinary studies, critically assessing their ability to grapple with the current phase of capitalist expansion. *Cultural Capitalism* resists the suggestion that politics is now merely 'cultural politics', but also challenges those who find the 'contamination' of politics by culture unacceptable.

Contributors: *Timothy Bewes, Jeremy Gilbert, Paul Smith, Martin McQuillan, Tiziana Terranova, Alan Finlayson, Matt Jordan, Karen Lisa Goldschmidt Salamon, Jo Littler.*